MATHS
NOW!
•••••••••••••
GET THE POINT!

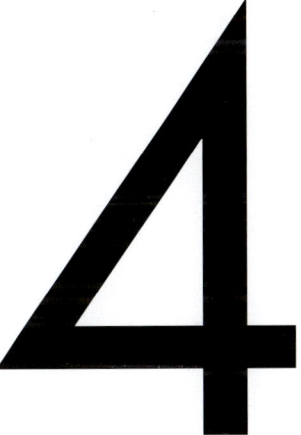

MATHS NOW!

GET THE POINT!

**TONY &
MARY ELLEN BELL**

JOHN MURRAY

Other titles in this series:

Maths Now! Get the Point! Pupil's 1	0 7195 7276 2
Maths Now! Get the Point! Teacher's Resource File 1	0 7195 7277 0
Maths Now! Get the Point! Pupil's 2	0 7195 7278 9
Maths Now! Get the Point! Teacher's Resource File 2	0 7195 7279 7
Maths Now! Get the Point! Pupil's 3	0 7195 7352 1
Maths Now! Get the Point! Teacher's Resource File 3	0 7195 7353 X

Forthcoming:

Maths Now! Get the Point! Pupil's 5	0 7195 7356 4
Maths Now! Get the Point! Teacher's Resource File 5	0 7195 7357 2
Maths Now! Get the Point! Pupil's 6	0 7195 7358 0
Maths Now! Get the Point! Teacher's Resource File 6	0 7195 7440 4

© Tony and Mary Ellen Bell 1999

First published in 1999
by John Murray (Publishers) Ltd
50 Albemarle Street
London W1X 4BD

All rights reserved. No part of this publication may be reproduced in any material form (including photocopying or storing in any medium by electronic means and whether or not transiently or incidentally to some other use of this publication) without the written permission of the publishers, except in accordance with the provisions of the Copyright, Designs and Patents Act 1988 or under the terms of a licence issued by the Copyright Licensing Agency.

Layouts by Stephen Rowling/unQualified Design.
Artwork by Tom Cross, Mike Flanagan, Mike Humphries, Janek Matysiak.
Cover design by John Townson/Creation.

Typeset in 12/14pt Times Roman by Wearset, Boldon, Tyne and Wear.
Printed and bound by G. Canale, Torino, Italy.

A CIP catalogue record for this book is available from the British Library.

ISBN 0 7195 7354 8
Teacher's Resource File 4 0 7195 7355 6

Contents

Acknowledgements — vi
How to use this book — vii

UNIT 1 Number – Place value to 10 000 — 1
UNIT 2 Handling data – Block, bar and bar-line graphs — 12
UNIT 3 Number – Addition up to 1000 — 21
UNIT 4 Shape and space – Angles and positions — 33
UNIT 5 Number – Multiplication by 2, 3, 4, 5, 6 and 10 — 45
UNIT 6 Shape and space – 2D and 3D shapes — 56
UNIT 7 Number – Decimal numbers to 2 decimal places — 66
UNIT 8 Measures – Length and weight — 80
UNIT 9 Number – Subtraction to 1000 — 93
UNIT 10 Measures – Area — 104
UNIT 11 Number – Division by 2, 3, 4, 5 and 10 — 113
UNIT 12 Measures – Time: duration of time and timetables — 125

Acknowledgements

Cover reproduced by courtesy of Dennis O'Clair/Tony Stone Images; **p.7** The Stock Market; **pp.29, 30, 36, 37** Last Resort Picture Library; **p.47** John Townson/Creation; **p.48** Last Resort Picture Library; **pp.50, 52, 53, 57, 58***l* John Townson/Creation; **p.58***r* Tony Bell; **p.59** Last Resort Picture Library; **pp.62, 63***t* John Townson/Creation; **pp.63***b*, **64** Last Resort Picture Library; **pp.66, 84** John Townson/Creation; **p.90***l* The Stock Market; **pp.90***r*, **91** John Townson/Creation; **p.99** Last Resort Picture Library; **p.101** Tony Bell; **p.104** John Townson/Creation; **p.109** Tony Bell; **pp.115, 120** Last Resort Picture Library; **p.122** BBC Television/Radio; **p.130** Dave Hogan All Action; **p.131** Tony Bell

t=top, *b*=bottom, *r*=right, *l*=left

The authors would like to thank Kim O'Driscoll, Researcher in low attainment in mathematics, University of Strathclyde, and all the schools and teachers throughout the country who helped in the development of this book.

How to use this book

This maths book is planned to help you understand and enjoy maths. You will be able to gain points which you will collect on a sheet so that you can see how well you are doing. You can swap these points for rewards.

In this book you will meet some symbols. They will tell you what you need and what to do. Here they are.

Work with a partner

Work in a group

See your teacher

Fetch equipment

Take a test

Stop and think

Copy and complete

When you **copy and complete**, replace a box ☐ with a number and a line _____ with a word or words.

Sometimes you are given an example to show you how to start. These are always written in red, like this.

We hope that you will enjoy this book.

1 Number

Place value to 10 000

Unit 1 words

zero	about	roughly
nearer to	thousand	hundred
value	greater than	between
equal	circle	digit

Remember

Examples are shown in red.

 means copy and complete.

 You need
- a set of Unit 1 vocabulary Snap cards.

 Play a game of Snap to help you learn the words.

 Try the **word test** to get some points.

1   What are these numbers **roughly** – to the nearest **ten**?

Remember

Keep your eye on the **tens** digit.

a) ①2 is roughly 10 .

b) 22 is roughly ☐ .

c) 32 is roughly ☐ .

d) 82 is roughly ☐ .

e) 23 is about ☐ .

f) 28 is about ☐ .

g) 25 is about ☐ .

h) 92 is about ☐ .

i) 96 is about ☐ .

j) 95 is about ☐ .

UNIT 1 NUMBER

2 What are these numbers **roughly** – to the nearest **hundred**?

a) ①20 is roughly 100 .

b) 220 is roughly ☐ .   c) 320 is roughly ☐ .
d) 820 is roughly ☐ .   e) 123 is about ☐ .
f) 323 is about ☐ .   g) 823 is about ☐ .
h) 150 is roughly ☐ .   i) 658 is roughly ☐ .
j) 858 is roughly ☐ .   k) 923 is about ☐ .
l) 950 is about ☐ .   m) 958 is about ☐ .

> **Remember**
>
> Keep your eye on the **hundreds** digit.
>
> Then look at the **tens** digit beside it.

3 You need

- base 10 blocks
- Worksheet 1 *Place Value Board*.

a) Put this number on your board.

Thousands	Hundreds	Tens	Units
	9	0	0

Use cubes to add **one hundred** and re-group.
Write down your answer.

b) Put this number on your board.

Thousands	Hundreds	Tens	Units
	9	9	0

Use cubes to add **one ten** and re-group.
Write down your answer.

Place value to 10 000   3

c) Put this number on your board.

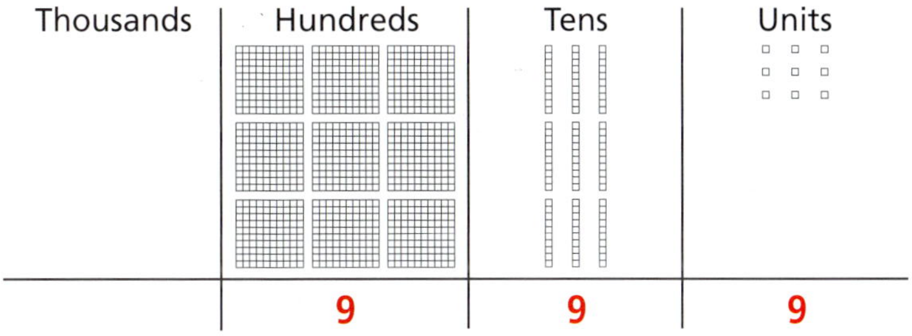

Thousands	Hundreds	Tens	Units
	9	9	9

 Use cubes to add **one unit** and re-group.
Write down your answer.

4 Fill in the missing numbers.
a) 100 200 300 ☐ ☐ ☐ 700 ☐ 900 ☐
b) 900 910 ☐ 930 ☐ 950 ☐ 970 ☐ 990 ☐
c) 990 991 ☐ 993 ☐ 995 ☐ 997 ☐ 999 ☐
d) 1000 900 ☐ ☐ ☐ 500 ☐ 300 ☐ 100
e) 1000 990 980 ☐ 960 ☐ 940 ☐ 920 ☐ 900
f) 1000 999 ☐ 997 ☐ 995 ☐ 993 ☐ 991 ☐

5 Are these numbers nearer to 1000 or nearer to 1100?
Use the number line below to help you.

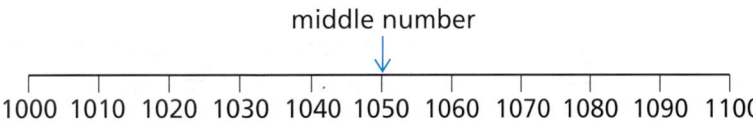

a) 1040 is nearer to ☐
b) 1020 is nearer to ☐
c) 1070 is nearer to ☐
d) 1010 is nearer to ☐
e) 1090 is nearer to ☐
f) 1030 is nearer to ☐

4   UNIT 1 NUMBER

 6   Try Worksheet 2 *Roughly (1)*.

7   What is the **value** of the circled digits:

  thousands, **hundreds**, **tens** or **units**?

  a) ⑦326,   7 thousands
  b) 7③26   c) 839④   d) 52①0   e) 1⑧65
  f) ⑨084   g) 170②   h) 6③40   i) ②396

8   Here is a table of some of the tallest mountains in the world.

Mountain	Height in metres
McKinley	6194
Blanc	4807
Everest	8848
Etna	3323
K2	8610
Kenya	5199
Ararat	5122

a) Match the **letter** to the **correct mountain** and write down the **height**.

  A,   Etna 3323 m

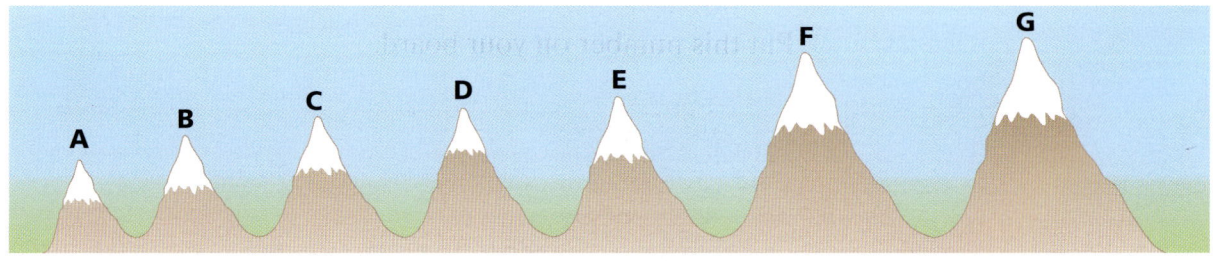

b) Write the mountains in **order of size – smallest** first.

c) The **highest** mountain is _____ .

Place value to 10 000   5

  9 You need

- base 10 blocks
- Worksheet 1 *Place Value Board*.

a) Put this number on your board.

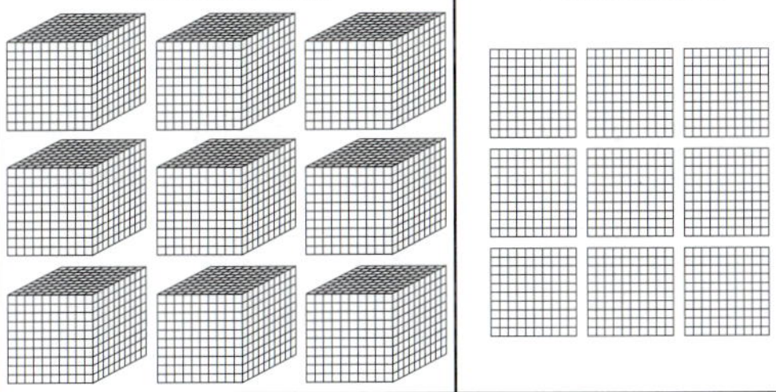

Ten Thousands	Thousands	Hundreds	Tens	Units
	9	9	0	0

 Use cubes to add **one hundred** and re-group. Write down your answer.

b) Put this number on your board.

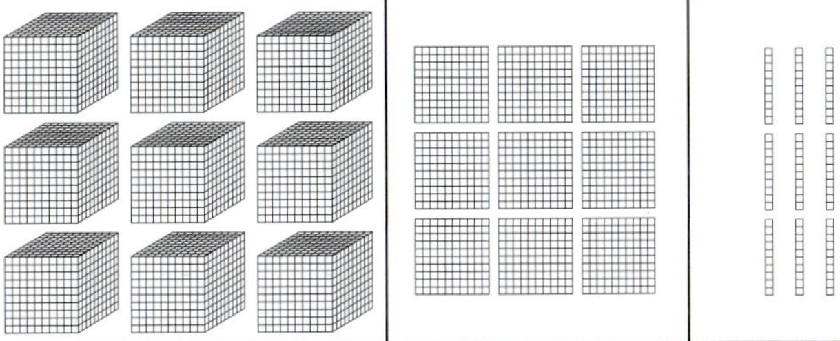

Ten Thousands	Thousands	Hundreds	Tens	Units
	9	9	9	0

 Use cubes to add **one ten** and re-group. Write down your answer.

c) Put this number on your board.

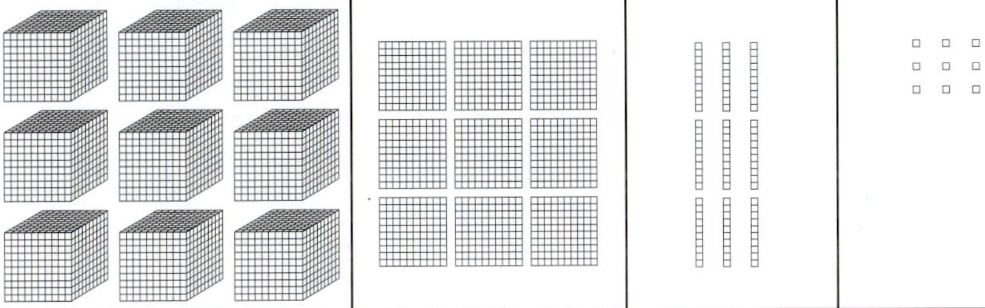

Ten Thousands	Thousands	Hundreds	Tens	Units
	9	9	9	9

 Use cubes to add **one unit** and re-group. Write down your answer.

UNIT 1 NUMBER

10 Write these numbers correctly with a space after the ten thousands.

> **Remember**
>
> When you write numbers, start at the **left** with the **largest** value. Leave a space **after** the **ten thousands**.
>
> 10 000

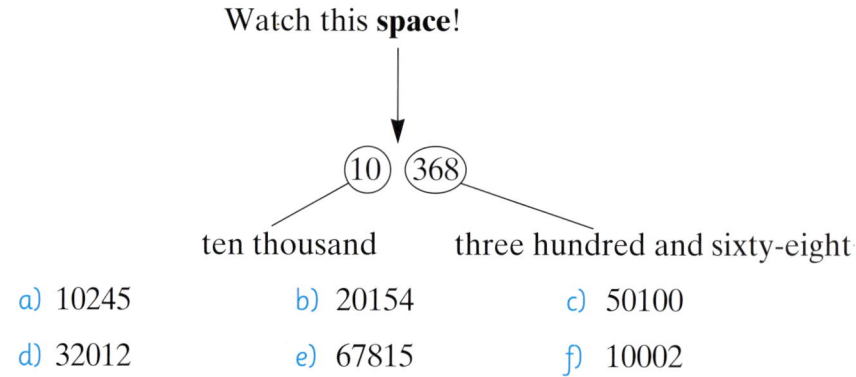

Watch this **space**!

(10) (368)

ten thousand   three hundred and sixty-eight

a) 10245   b) 20154   c) 50100

d) 32012   e) 67815   f) 10002

11 Write in numbers.

> **Remember**
>
> When a number is **10 000 or more** there must be a **space** and **three** digits after the **thousands**.

a) Ten thousand six hundred and forty-three

b) Ten thousand six hundred and forty

c) Ten thousand and forty-three

d) Ten thousand six hundred and three

e) Ten thousand and three

Place value to 10 000

12 Eve works in a bank.

She groups and changes money like this.

 changes for

 changes for

 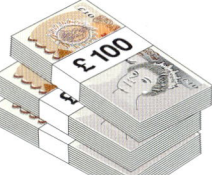  changes for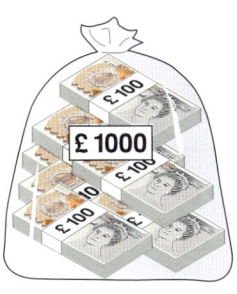

Which is worth **most**:
one £1 coin, one £10 note,
one bundle of £100 or one bag of £1000?

a) One _____ is worth most.

b) One _____ has the biggest value.

Which is worth **least**?

c) One _____ is worth least.

d) One _____ has the least value.

UNIT 1 NUMBER

   e) How many bags of £1000 do you think Eve will put in this big bag?

 13 Try Worksheets 3 and 4 *Bank it (1)* and *(2)*.

 14 How many **digits** are there in these numbers?

a) 8 = ☐ digit   b) 642 = ☐ digits   c) 3145 = ☐ digits

d) 98 = ☐ digits   e) 10 213 = ☐ digits

f) The **smallest** number is ☐.

g) Put all the numbers in order – **smallest** number first.

15 Write these numbers in words:

a) 10 327   b) 10 300   c) 10 027   d) 10 320   e) 10 007

 16 Write these words in numbers.

a) Ten thousand three hundred = ☐

b) Ten thousand three hundred and forty = ☐

c) Ten thousand and six = ☐

d) Ten thousand three hundred and forty-six = ☐

> **Remember**
> Leave a **space**.

> **Remember**
> **Total** means **add**.

17 Find the **total**.

a) 10 000 + 200 + 40 = ☐ 10 240 ☐

b) 10 000 + 200 + 40 + 5 = ☐

c) 10 000 + 200 = ☐

d) 10 000 + 40 = ☐

e) 10 000 + 5 = ☐

f) 10 000 + 40 + 5 = ☐

g) 10 000 + 200 + 5 = ☐

Place value to 10 000

 18 Try Worksheet 5 *One value*.

19 Each arrow below points to one of these numbers.
Match each arrow to the correct **number**.

| 9150 | 9740 | 9970 | 9060 | 9910 |
| 9430 | 9250 | 9560 | 9690 | 9340 |

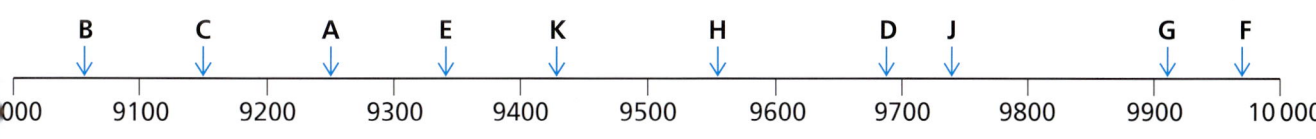

Arrow **A** points to 9250.

 20 Try Worksheet 6 *Roughly (2)*.

 21 Try Worksheet 7 *Move back*.

  **22** Try Worksheet Puzzle *Card game*.

  23 You need
- Unit 1 Race against time cards
- your 'My maths record' sheet.

Race against time

1 Sort the race cards – this side up.
Take the cards one at a time.
Answer as quickly as you can.

2 Look at the other side of the card for the answer.

 3 When you get all the answers correct, ask a friend to test you.

4 Now **Race against time**.
Go for points!
Ask your teacher to test and time you.

1⃝0 653

ten thousands

Remember
3 errors = 1 point   2 errors = 2 points
1 error = 3 points   0 errors = 5 points
Answer in 1 minute with 0 errors = 7 points

 Now try Unit 1 Test.

Review 1

1. Copy and shade the **columns** to show the following number of people. Look carefully at each scale.

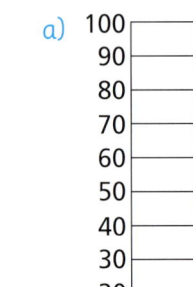
a) 75 people

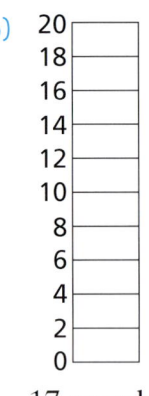
b) 17 people

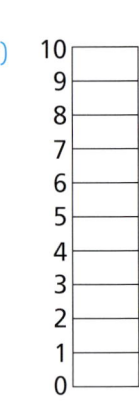
c) 5 people

2. a) 4p + 5p = ☐ b) 14p + 5p = ☐
   c) 3p + 5p = ☐ d) 13p + 5p = ☐
   e) 5p + 6p = ☐ f) 15p + 6p = ☐
   g) 8p + 7p = ☐ h) 18p + 7p = ☐

3. How much rock in each picture? Write as a decimal.

a)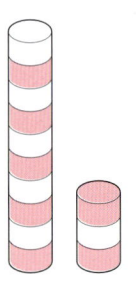
b)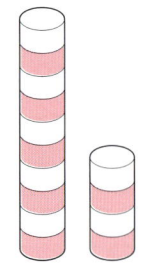
c)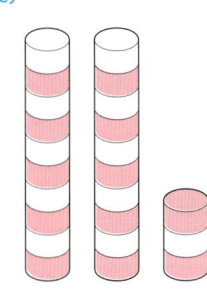

a) ☐.☐   b) ☐.☐   c) ☐.☐

4. Choose the correct unit of measure – **grams (g)** or **kilograms (kg)**.

a) We weigh mushrooms in _____ .

b) We weigh potatoes in _____ .

5 What is **half** ($\frac{1}{2}$) of each of these weights?

    a) 12 kg   b) 20 kg   c) 18 kg   d) 6 kg   e) 8 kg

    f) 10 kg   g) 4 kg   h) 16 kg   i) 14 kg   j) 2 kg

6 Which decimal is nearest to 1 whole?

    0.2   0.9   0.5   0.1   0.3   0.6

2 Handling data

Block, bar and bar-line graphs

Unit 2 words

bar-line	guess	impossible
likely	unlikely	certain
half-way	block graph	scale
different	same	less than

Remember

Examples are shown in red.

 means copy and complete.

 You need
- a set of Unit 2 vocabulary Snap cards.

 Play a game of Snap to help you learn the words.

 Try the **word test** to get some points.

1   How many people does each **coloured column** stand for? Look carefully at each scale.

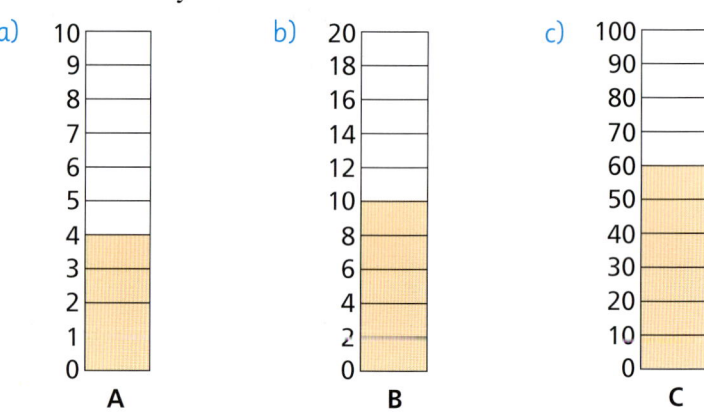

a) Column A shows ☐ people. ☐ blocks are coloured.

Block, bar and bar-line graphs 13

b) Column B shows ☐ people. ☐ blocks are coloured.

c) Column C shows ☐ people. ☐ blocks are coloured.

2 How many people does each **coloured bar** stand for? Look carefully at each scale.

Bar A
0 2 4 6 8 10 12 14 16 18 20

Bar B
0 10 20 30 40 50 60 70 80 90 100

Bar C
0 1 2 3 4 5 6 7 8 9 10

a) Bar A shows ☐ people.

b) Bar B shows ☐ people.

c) Bar C shows ☐ people.

3 Try Worksheet 1 *More scales*.

4 Look at the two graphs below.

Block graph of popular trainers

Bar chart of popular trainers

a) On the **block** graph ☐ people wore **Slobbi** trainers.
On the **bar** chart ☐ people wore **Slobbi** trainers.

b) On the **block** graph ☐ people wore **Flash** trainers.
On the **bar** chart ☐ people wore **Flash** trainers.

c) On the **block** graph, **most** people wore _____ trainers.
On the **bar** chart, **most** people wore _____ trainers.

d) On the **block** graph, **fewest** people wore _____ trainers.
On the **bar** chart, **fewest** people wore _____ trainers.

e) What do you notice about the two graphs?

UNIT 2 HANDLING DATA

5 This graph is called a **bar-line graph**.

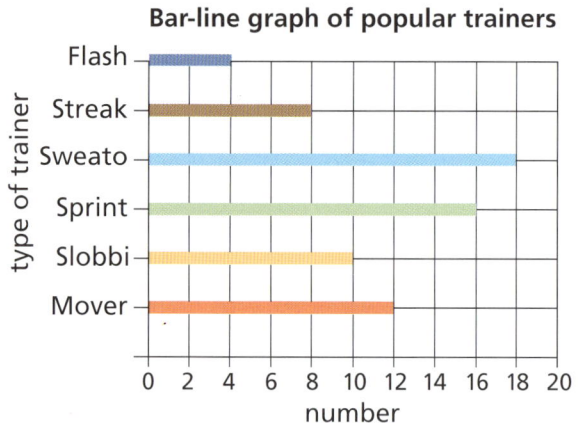

a) ☐ people wore **Slobbi** trainers.

b) ☐ people wore **Flash** trainers.

c) **Most** people wore _____ trainers.

d) **Fewest** people wore _____ trainers.

e) Look at your answers to the **Questions 4** and **5**.
What do you notice?
How do bar charts and bar-line graphs look different?

6 Try Worksheets 2 and 3 *More graphs (1)* and *(2)*.

7 A group of teenagers were asked where they went on holidays.
Here is the **tally table** of their answers.

Holiday	Tally marks	Total
Home	|||| |||| ||||	
Away in Britain	|||| |||| |||| ||||	
Spain	|||| ||	
France	|||	
America	||||	
Other	||	

a) Copy and complete the tally table or

Block, bar and bar-line graphs   15

b) Copy the grid below on to squared paper (or 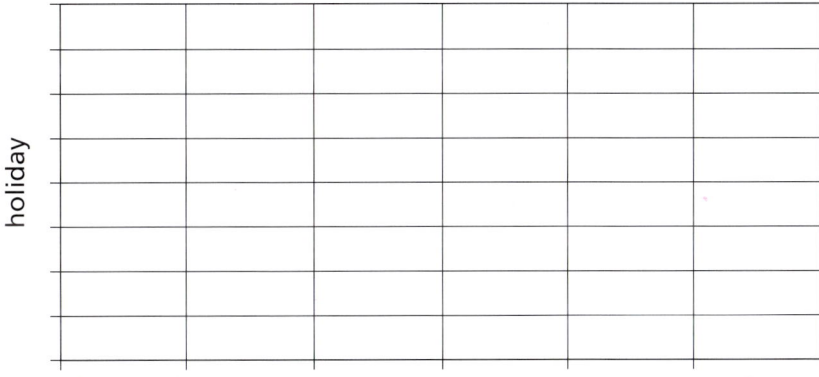).

Use it to draw a **bar-line graph** to show where the teenagers went on holiday.

Remember

You can use one block to stand for 1 or 2 people.

(grid with y-axis labelled "holiday" and x-axis labelled "number")

8 A **bigger** group of people were asked where they went on holidays.
Here is the **tally table** of their answers.

Holiday	Tally marks	Total	Total roughly
Home	IIII IIII IIII IIII IIII IIII IIII IIII IIII IIII IIII II		
Away in Britain	IIII IIII IIII IIII IIII IIII IIII IIII IIII IIII IIII IIII IIII IIII		
Spain	IIII IIII IIII IIII IIII		
France	IIII IIII II		
America	IIII IIII IIII IIII IIII		
Other	IIII I		

a) Copy and complete the tally table or

You must fill in the **'total roughly'** column to the **nearest ten**.

Remember

You can use one block to stand for 1 or 2 or 10 people.

b) Use the grid in **Question 7** and copy it on to squared paper (or).

Using results from the **'total roughly'** column, show the table above as a **bar-line graph**.

9 How many people if 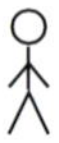 = 10 people?

a) 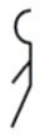 = ☐ people

b) 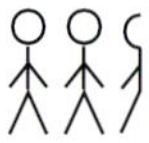 = ☐ people

c) 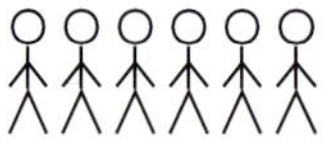 = ☐ people

10 Look at the results of the holiday survey in **Question 8**. Using the **'total roughly'** results, make a **pictogram** where 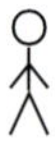 = 10 people.

Remember

Rules for drawing a pictogram

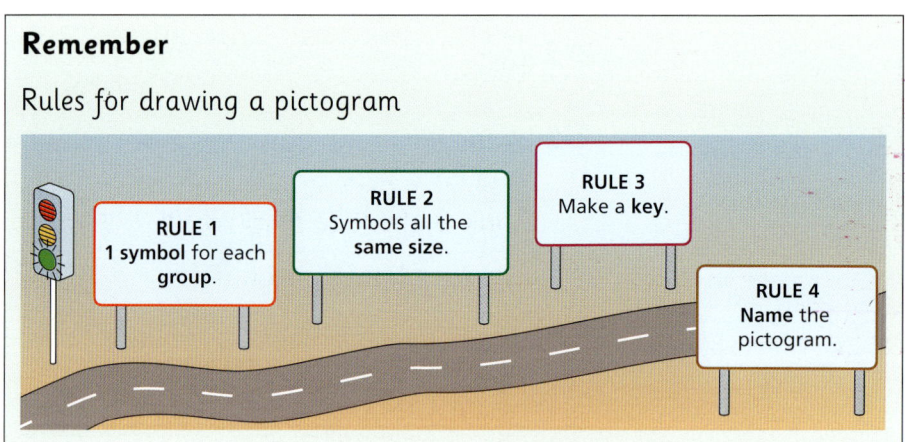

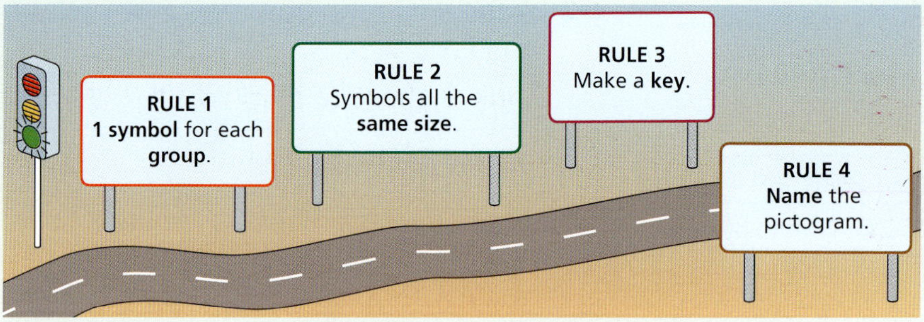
RULE 1
1 symbol for each group.
RULE 2
Symbols all the same size.
RULE 3
Make a key.
RULE 4
Name the pictogram.

11 How sure are you that the events below will take place?

Remember

When we make a **guess** we can often use words to describe how sure we are that events **will** or **will not** happen.

from -- to

impossible — unlikely — likely — certain

a) It is ____________________ that it will snow in January.

b) It is ____________________ that it will snow in May.

c) It is ____________________ that it will rain pennies tomorrow.

d) It is ____________________ that the sun will shine again.

Block, bar and bar-line graphs   17

12 On a line numbered like the one below, match these words to a number.

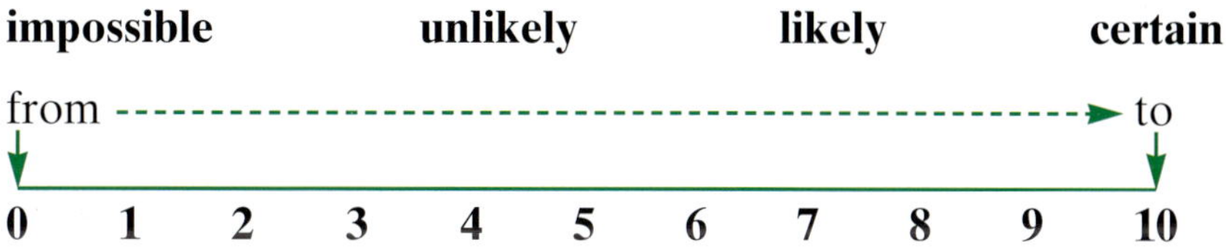

| impossible | unlikely | likely | certain |

from --→ to

0 1 2 3 4 5 6 7 8 9 10

a) impossible   `0`

b) unlikely   ☐

c) likely   ☐

d) certain   ☐

 13 Try Worksheet 6 *How sure?*

14 Can you think of some 'describing' sentences to place **half-way** along the number line – beside the 5? Look at these to help you.

The next baby born to-day will be a girl.

If I drop a coin it will land 'head up'.

I will lift my right glove first.

UNIT 2 HANDLING DATA

 15 From the sentences below, write down those which could also be placed on the number line – beside the 5.

   a) My baby brother will grow taller as he gets older.

   b) If my friend chooses a number between 1 and 100, it will be an odd number.

   c) If I pick any card from a full pack of cards, it will be red.

   d) The next sunny day will be on a Monday.

16 Look at the list of places in the table below.

Holiday places		Tally marks	Total
A	Mountains		
B	Sea-side		
C	Lakes		
D	City		
E	Home		
F	Country		

If you asked all the people in your class this question, what do you think their answers would be?
(They can each choose only **one** holiday.)

 a) Copy the number line below or

Guess the results of the survey. For example, if you think '**Home**' will be the **least popular**, you arrow the **E** to the **zero**.

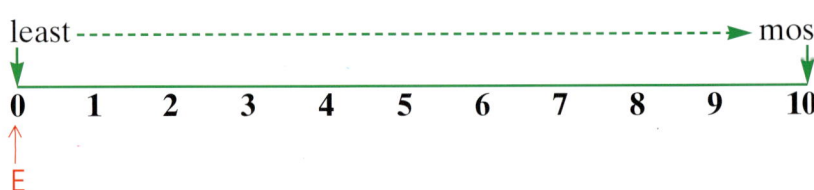

Block, bar and bar-line graphs 19

b) Now do the survey and complete the tally table opposite.

c) Use squared paper to show your results on a bar-line graph.

d) Look at your guesses on the number line.
Talk about how close your guesses were.

Now try Unit 2 Test.

Review 2

1. What is the value of the circled digit – **thousands**, **hundreds**, **tens** or **units**?

    a) 6(1)5   b) (1)056   c) 56(1)   d) (1)659

2. a) 4 7
      + 3 2
      ─────

   b) 5 7
      + 4 3
      ─────

   c) 9 7
      + 9 4
      ─────

   d) 2 8 8
      +   6 2
      ─────

3. a) 2 + 2 + 2 + 2 + 2 + 2 = ☐   6 × 2 = ☐

   b) 5 + 5 + 5 + 5 + 5 + 5 + 5 + 5 = ☐   8 × 5 = ☐

   c) 10 + 10 + 10 + 10 = ☐   4 × 10 = ☐

4. What fraction is shaded? Write as a fraction and as a decimal.

   a)

   b)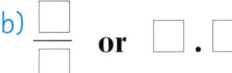

   a) ☐/☐ or ☐.☐   b) ☐/☐ or ☐.☐

5. a) £17 − £8 = ☐   b) £27 − £8 = ☐
   c) £47 − £8 = ☐   d) £97 − £8 = ☐

6. Put these periods of time in order – **shortest** time first.

   ¼ hour   60 minutes   half an hour   45 minutes   two hours

7. Put these times in order – **earliest** time first.

   A   B   C   D
      Half past one   1 : 45   quarter to one

3 Number

Addition: up to 1000

Unit 3 words

order	number lines	calculator
nearest ten	**nearest hundred**	more than
less than	middle number	value
coins	large	group

> **Remember**
> Examples are shown in red.
>
> means copy and complete.

 You need
- a set of Unit 3 vocabulary Snap cards.

 Play a game of Snap to help you learn the words.

 Try the **word test** to get some points.

 1 a) 2 + 6 + 8 = ☐   b) 3 + 5 + 7 = ☐
c) 7 + 4 + 7 = ☐   d) 9 + 2 + 5 = ☐
e) 5 + 5 + 5 + 2 = ☐   f) 1 + 7 + 9 + 3 = ☐

 You need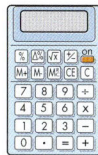
- a calculator.

g) Check your answers on the calculator.

 h) Put the numbers into the calculator in different orders. Do the answers change?

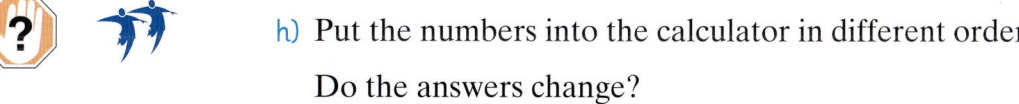

22   UNIT 3 NUMBER

i) Can you think of any easy ways to add the numbers above **in your head**?

2 + 6 + 8 could be done as 2 + 8 + 6.

Which is easier? Why?

 2 Write down the numbers 1 to 10.

a) Try to find as many groups as you can of **three** different numbers which add up to **20**.

3 + 8 + 9 = 20

b) Try to find as many groups as you can of **three** different numbers which add up to **more than 20**.

7 + 8 + 9 = 24

Who found the most numbers?

 3 Lee set out the sum 143 + 15 in columns to help him to work out the answer.

```
  143
+  15
-----
  293
```

His answer, **293**, is **wrong**.

Tell your partner or teacher where Lee went wrong.

 4 a) £8 + £6 = ☐   b) £18 + £6 = ☐

c) £6 + £7 = ☐   d) £16 + £7 = ☐

e) £5 + £9 = ☐   f) £15 + £9 = ☐

g) £9 + £5 = ☐   h) £19 + £5 = ☐

 5 a) 4p + 5p = ☐   b) 14p + 5p = ☐

c) 24p + 5p = ☐   d) 54p + 5p = ☐

e) 7p + 6p = ☐   f) 17p + 6p = ☐

g) 27p + 6p = ☐   h) 66p + 7p = ☐

i) 9p + 5p = ☐   j) 19p + 5p = ☐

k) 39p + 5p = ☐   l) 59p + 5p = ☐

Addition: up to 1000 23

 6 Try Worksheet 1 *Bags of money*.

  7 You need

- Worksheet 2 *Money cards*.

Shuffle the money cards and place them face down.
Take turns to pick a card.
When you have **three** cards which add up to **£1**
make one set and keep them.
The person who makes most sets is the winner.

 8 Copy the number line.
Draw in the arrow and complete.

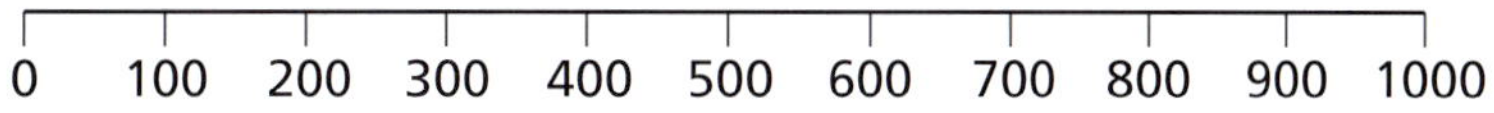

```
 0   100  200  300  400  500  600  700  800  900  1000
```

100 + 300 = ☐

 9 You need

- base 10 blocks to show how you add and regroup.

a) 150 + 70 = ☐   b) 156 + 76 = ☐

   c) Explain how you did these to your partner or teacher.

 10 a) H T U   b) H T U   c) H T U
        1 4 7   1 8 0   1 6 6
      +1 1 8   +   6 0   +   7 5

d) H T U   e) H T U
    3 3 8   5 7 5
  +1 8 9   +3 5 7

24 UNIT 3 NUMBER

> **Remember**
> Only one digit in each column

 11 You need
- a *Place Value Board*
- base 10 blocks.

Put these numbers on your board.
Write down the sum and work out the answer.

 a)

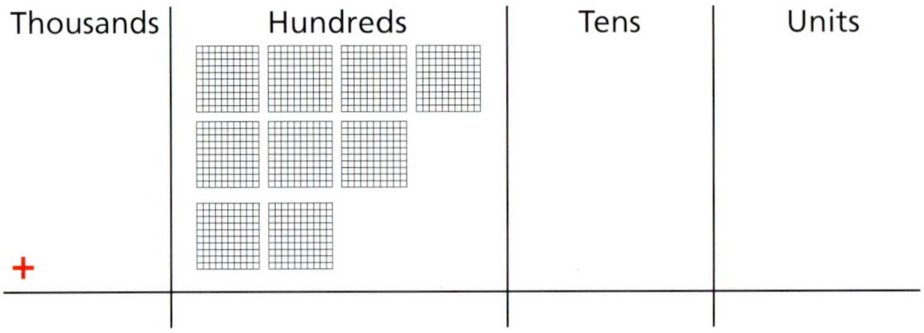

 b)

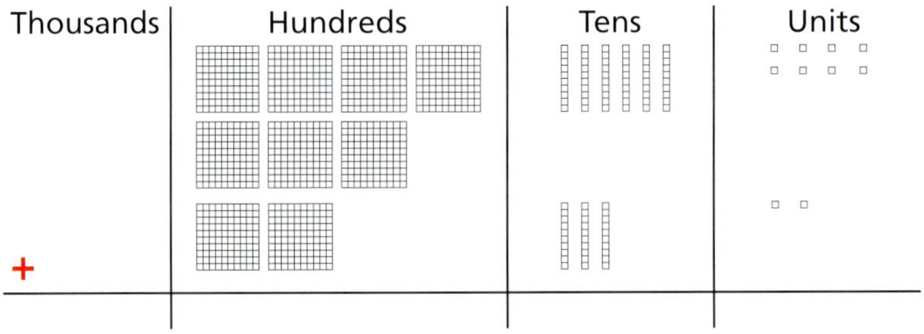

 12 Try Worksheet 3 *Group the hundreds*.

 13 Copy the number line.
Draw in the arrow and complete.

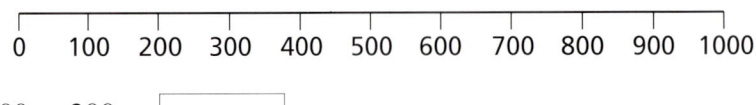

700 + 300 = ☐

 14 a) 200 + 800 = ☐   b) 800 + 200 = ☐

c) 600 + 400 = ☐   d) 700 + 300 = ☐

e) 100 + 900 = ☐   f) 500 + 500 = ☐

Addition: up to 1000   25

 15 Look at the drawings to help you with the sums.

> **Remember**
>
> **Ten boxes of 100 biscuits = 1 box of 1000 biscuits**
>
> 10 groups of a **hundred** = 1 group of a **thousand**

a)

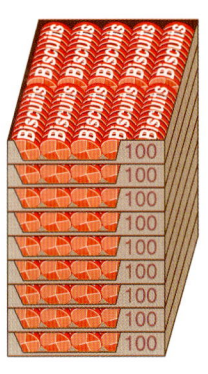

```
Th H T U
    9 0 0
+   1 0 0
─────────
  □ □ □ □
  □
```

b)

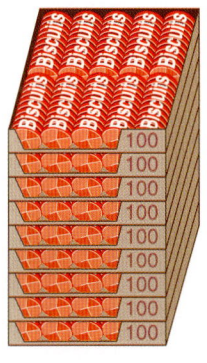

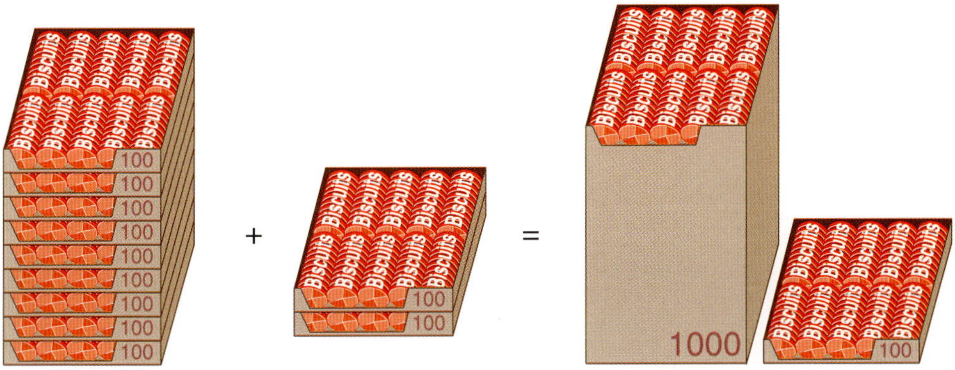

```
Th H T U
    9 0 0
+   □ □ □
─────────
  □ □ □ □
  □
```

c)

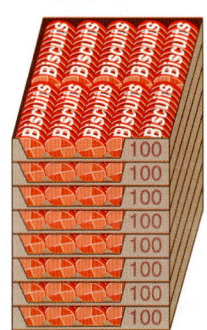

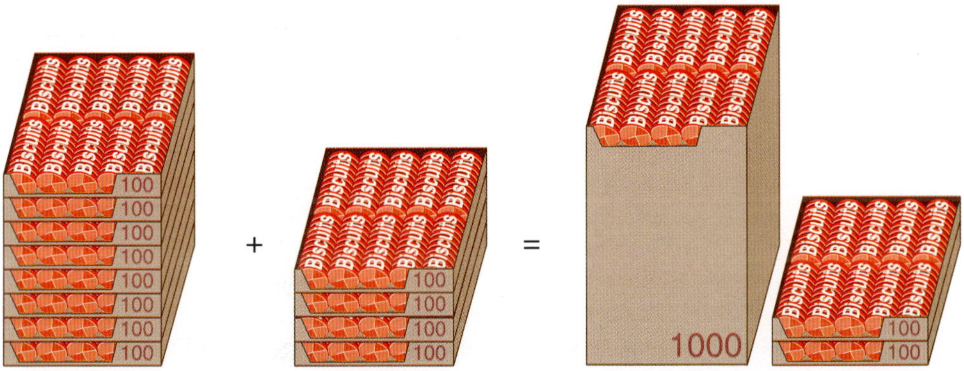

```
Th H T U
    □ □ □
+   □ □ □
─────────
  □ □ □ □
  □
```

26 UNIT 3 NUMBER

16 Add these numbers.

a)   1 3 6
   +   3 1
   ———

b)   2 6
   + 8 4
   ———

c)   2 0 6
   +   1 4
   ———

d)   2 8 6
   +   7 4
   ———

e)   2 4 5
   + 1 1 2
   ———

f)   1 9 9
   + 7 9 9
   ———

Remember

Check if you need to carry.

17 Try Worksheet 4 *Jigsaw addition*.

18 Add these numbers.
Then write them to the **nearest hundred** and add.

```
   1 2 0          1 0 0
 + 2 1 0        + 2 0 0
 ———            ———
   3 3 0          3 0 0
```

a)   2 4 0
   + 3 5 0

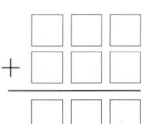

+

b)   2 6 0
   + 3 7 0

+

c)   5 2 8
   + 1 7 2

+

d)   5 5 3
   + 4 4 7

+

19 Ella works in a shop for four weeks over the summer holidays.
She counts the money taken on Fridays and Saturdays.

Guess the total taken each Friday and Saturday.
(Look at the amounts to the **nearest hundred**.)
Then work out the answer.

Addition: up to 1000   27

Week 1
Money taken on Friday.   Money taken on Saturday.

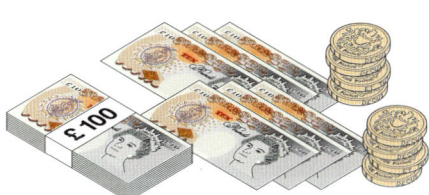 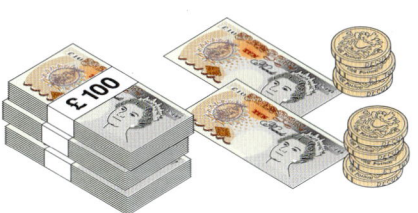

a) I guess the answer will be about £☐ .

b) Altogether £☐ was taken on Friday and Saturday.

Week 2
Money taken on Friday.   Money taken on Saturday.

 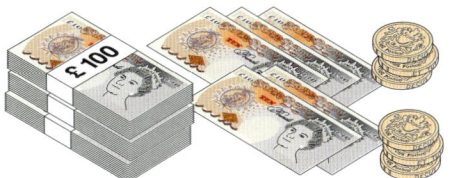

c) I guess the answer will be about £☐ .

d) Altogether £☐ was taken on Friday and Saturday.

Week 3
Money taken on Friday.   Money taken on Saturday.

e) I guess the answer will be about £☐ .

f) Altogether £☐ was taken on Friday and Saturday.

g) Most money was taken on week ☐ .

h) Least money was taken on week ☐ .

UNIT 3 NUMBER

20 Pick out the **odd** numbers and add them together.

a) 2   4   5   6   8   9

b) 52   54   55   56   58   59

c) 152   154   155   156   158   159

d) What do you notice about your answers?
Are they odd or even numbers?

21 Pick out the **even** numbers and add them together.

a) 2   3   5   7   8   9

b) 42   43   45   47   48   49

c) 642   643   645   647   348   649

d) What do you notice about your answers?
Are they odd or even numbers?

 22 You need

- a calculator.

Find the missing answers, and complete the patterns.

a)
3 + 6 = ☐
13 + 6 = ☐
23 + 6 = ☐
33 + 6 = ☐
43 + 6 = ☐
☐ + ☐ = ☐
☐ + ☐ = ☐

b)
113 + 6 = ☐
213 + 6 = ☐
313 + 6 = ☐
413 + 6 = ☐
513 + 6 = ☐
☐ + ☐ = ☐
☐ + ☐ = ☐

c)
16 + 14 = ☐
26 + 14 = ☐
36 + 14 = ☐
46 + 14 = ☐
56 + 14 = ☐
☐ + ☐ = ☐
☐ + ☐ = ☐

Addition: up to 1000   29

23 These people want to buy cars when they are older.
They know it will take a few years to save up the money.

a) Kate did these summer holiday jobs to get money.

Income = £136   Income = £178

Kate got £ ⬚ altogether.

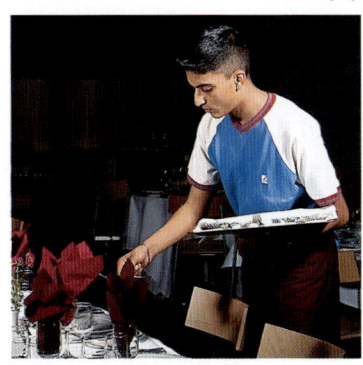

b) Patrick did these holiday jobs to get money.

Income = £145   Income = £189

Patrick got ⬚ altogether.

c) Joe did these holiday jobs to get money.

Income = £197   Income = £118

Joe got a total of £ ⬚ .

UNIT 3 NUMBER

d) Ella did these summer holiday jobs to get money.

Income = £136   Income = £199

d) Ella got a total of ☐ .

e) _____ got the most money?

f) _____ got the least money?

g) Put the names with the totals in order, **smallest** first.

24 Try Worksheet 5 *Problem page*.

25 Try Worksheet Puzzle *Money*.

Now try Unit 3 Test.

Review 3

1. What are these numbers roughly to the nearest hundred?
   a) 320 is roughly ☐. b) 1320 is roughly ☐.
   c) 10 320 is roughly ☐. d) 481 is about ☐.
   e) 2431 is about ☐. f) 10 451 is about ☐.

2. a) Fill in the missing numbers.

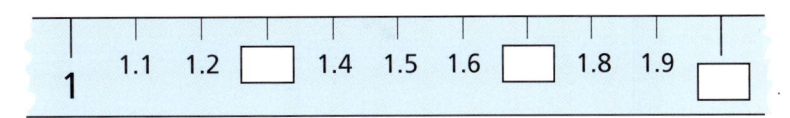

   1   1.1   1.2   ☐   1.4   1.5   1.6   ☐   1.8   1.9   ☐

   b) Write in order – smallest decimal first.

   4.8   0.8   0.4   8.0

3. Measure the lines in centimetres.

   a) _____

   b) _____

4. a) ☐ × 5 = 20   b) 35 ÷ 5 = ☐   c) 25 ÷ 5 = ☐
   d) 40 ÷ 5 = ☐   e) ☐ × 5 = 15   f) 45 ÷ 5 = ☐

5. Write the **24-hour** clock times for these 12-hour times. The two dots : separate the hours from the minutes.

   a) 3.00 p.m. = 15:00

   b) 5.00 p.m.   c) 8.00 p.m.   d) 1.00 p.m.

   e) 11.00 p.m.   f) 7.00 p.m.   g) 4.00 p.m.

6. Copy and label the points on this compass, S, E and W.

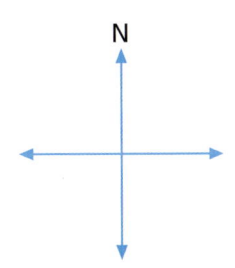

7 How many ¼ turns, **clockwise** or **anticlockwise**?

a) ☐ ¼ turn _____

b) ☐ ¼ turns _____

c) ☐ ¼ turns _____

4 Shape and space

Angles and positions

Unit 4 words

acute	obtuse	bottom
side	co-ordinates	right angle
North (N)	South (S)	East (E)
West (W)	direction	zero

Remember

Examples are shown in red.

✏ means copy and complete.

You need
- a set of Unit 4 vocabulary Snap cards.

Play a game of Snap to help you learn the words.

Try the **word test** to get some points.

1

Remember

This is a **right angle**.

Here are two more angles.

Angle **less than** a right angle   Angle **greater than** a right angle

A **sharp** pointed angle   A **blunt** angle

UNIT 4 SHAPE AND SPACE

Choose the word **sharp** or **blunt** for these angles.

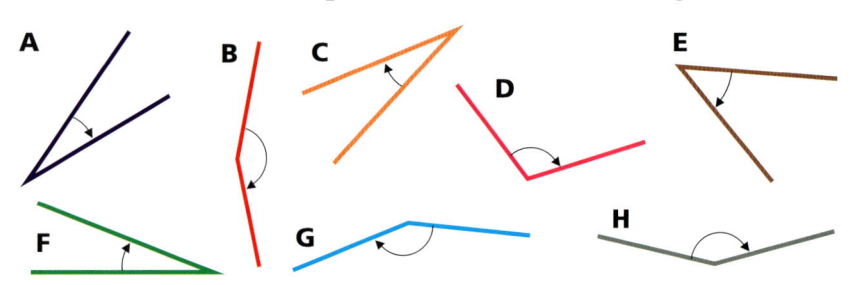

A is a sharp angle.

2 Look at the angles of these roof tops.

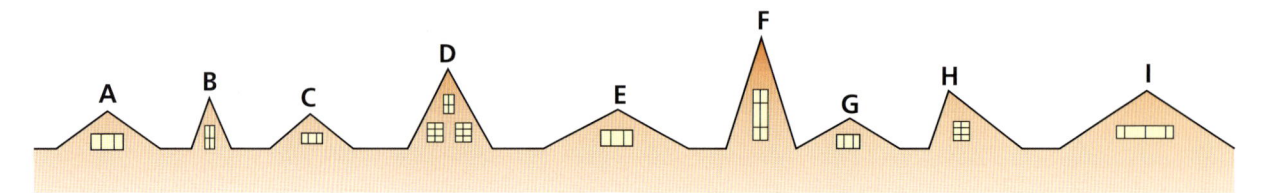

Choose the word **acute** or **obtuse** for each angle.

A is an obtuse angle.   B is an acute angle.

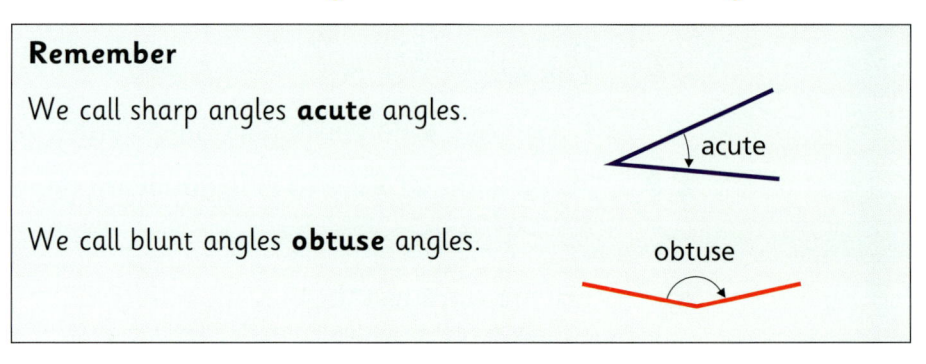

Remember

We call sharp angles **acute** angles.

We call blunt angles **obtuse** angles.

3 Can you think of a way to remember which is **acute** and which **obtuse**?

Here is one way. Sometimes people say they have **acute** pain.

I have acute pain in my tum!

Angles and positions 35

4 Try Worksheet 1 *Colour the angles*.

5 What angles do these clock hands move through:

acute, **obtuse** or **right angle**?

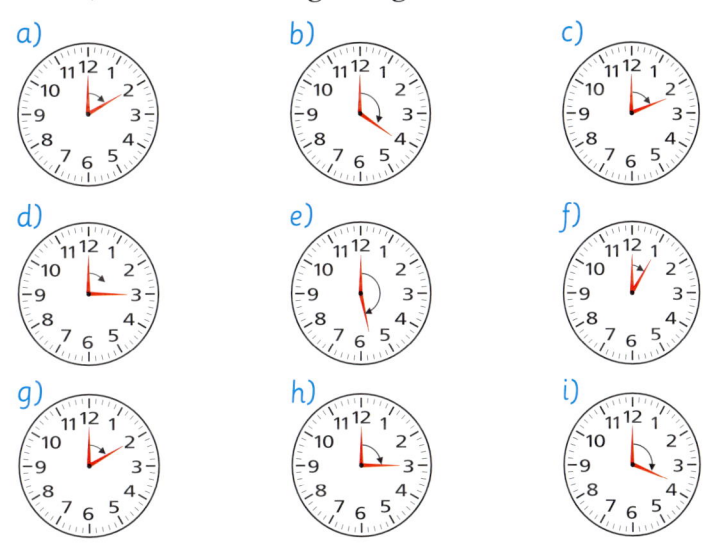

a)   b)   c)

d)   e)   f)

g)   h)   i)

a) acute

6 You need

- geostrips, meccano strips or card strips fastened at one end.

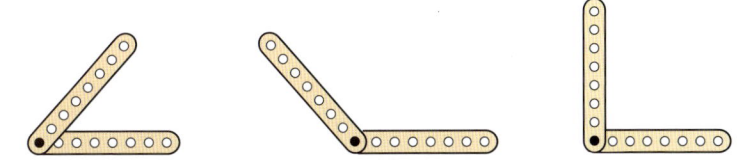

Make an **acute**,   **obtuse**   and **right angle**
with your angle maker.
Draw them on paper and write **acute**, **obtuse** or **right angle** in each angle.

7 Try Worksheets 2 and 3 *Cut and sort (1) and (2)*.

8 You need

- squared paper or

Try a game of *Copy the coloured squares*.

a) **Players A** and **B** each draw a big square – 6 small squares by 6 small squares.

UNIT 4 SHAPE AND SPACE

b) **Player A** colours 1 small square red, 1 blue and 1 green.

c) **Player A** says which squares he/she has coloured.

d) **Player B** tries to colour the same squares on his/her paper.

> Player A does **not** show the coloured squares to Player B.
>
> Player A does **not** look at Player B's work until he/she has finished.

e) Did **Player B** put each coloured square in the right place?

f) Players can now change over and play the game again.

9 We can show squares on a grid using **letters** and **numbers**. The **red** square is found by going along to **C** and up to **5** – **C5**.

Remember

The rule is we go **along the bottom** first.

Then **up the side**.

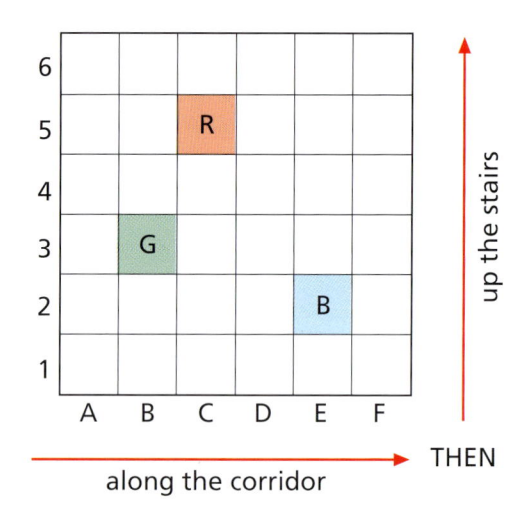

along the corridor THEN up the stairs

Remember

You go **along the corridor** – then **up the stairs**.

Along the corridor and up the stairs

a) The red square is at <u>C5</u>.

b) The blue square is at _____ .

c) The green square is at _____ .

Angles and positions 37

d) Use letters and numbers to play another game of *Copy the coloured squares*.

e) Why do you think it was easier to play the game this time?

10 Sam joins his friends at the cinema.
He looks for his seat.

First he finds the **letter** on the row.
Then he finds the **number** of his seat.
Sam's seat is at **A4** – this means Row A, Seat 4.

Who is sitting on these seats?

a) Jack is sitting on B4.

b) B5 c) C3 d) D4 e) C2 f) B3

g) A3 h) C5 i) B1 j) C4 k) D2

l) Write down the letters and numbers of the **empty** seats.

11 Kate, Pat, Ella and Joe go for a trip to the town of Beeny.

UNIT 4 SHAPE AND SPACE

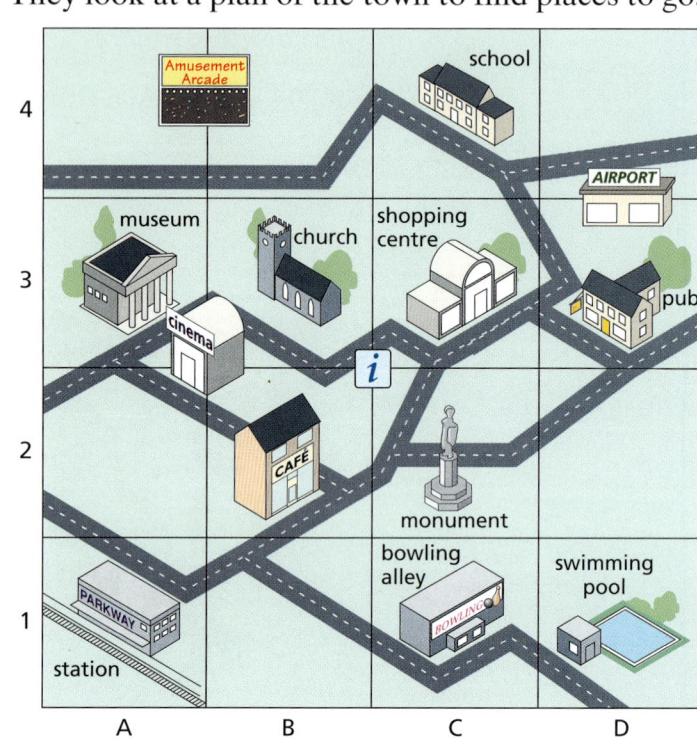

They look at a plan of the town to find places to go.

Where would they visit if they picked places in these squares?

a) The pool is in square D1.

b) The _____ is in square D3.

c) The _____ is in square C4.

d) The _____ is in square C2.

e) The _____ is in square B2.

f) The _____ is in square A1.

12 In which square on the plan would you find these places?

a) The shopping centre is in C3.

b) The museum is in _____ .

c) The church is in _____ .

d) The station is in _____ .

e) The bowling alley is in _____ .

f) Find some places which are not completely **in** a square. How could you describe where they are?

Angles and positions **39**

13 The **cinema** and the **airport** are not in squares.
We can add more lines to place them better:

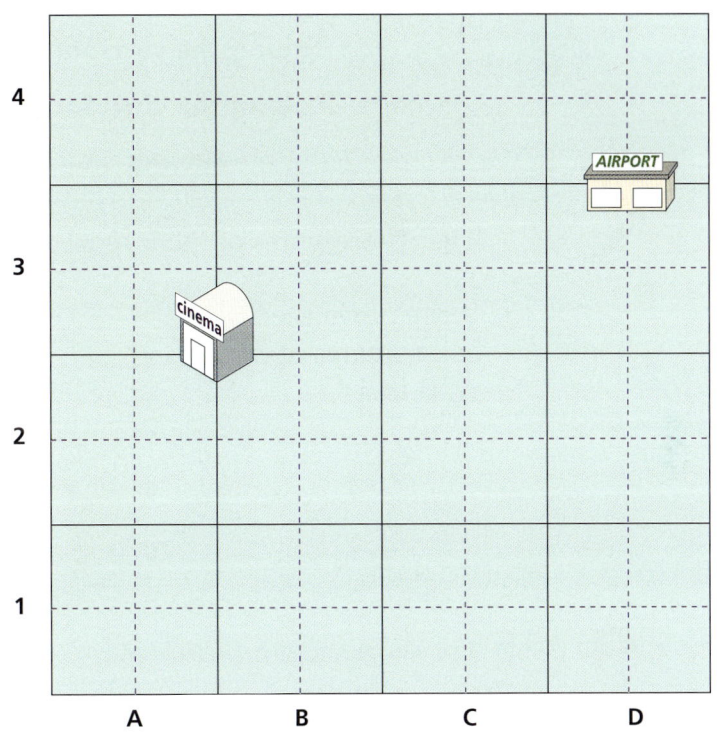

We number the lines like this.

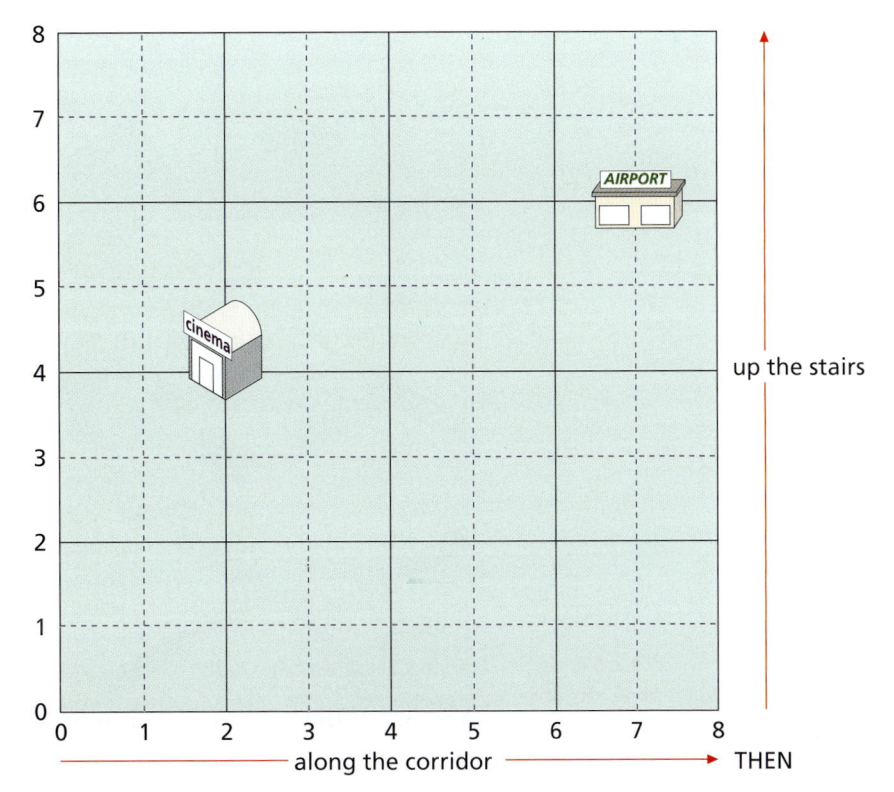

Remember

Both lines start with zero.

up the stairs

along the corridor → THEN

UNIT 4 SHAPE AND SPACE

> **Remember**
>
> We say pairs of numbers or **co-ordinates** like this:
>
> (**along the corridor**,   **up the stairs**)
>
> The cinema is (**2 along the corridor** and **4 up the stairs**).
>
> The co-ordinates of the **cinema** are (**2, 4**).

The co-ordinates of the airport are (,).

14 Write down the co-ordinates of A, B and C.

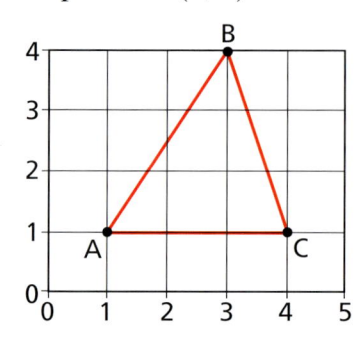

15 Try Worksheet 6 *Picture it*.

16 Kate, Pat, Ella and Joe go for another visit to Beeny. They call at the tourist information office. They plan a day around the town.

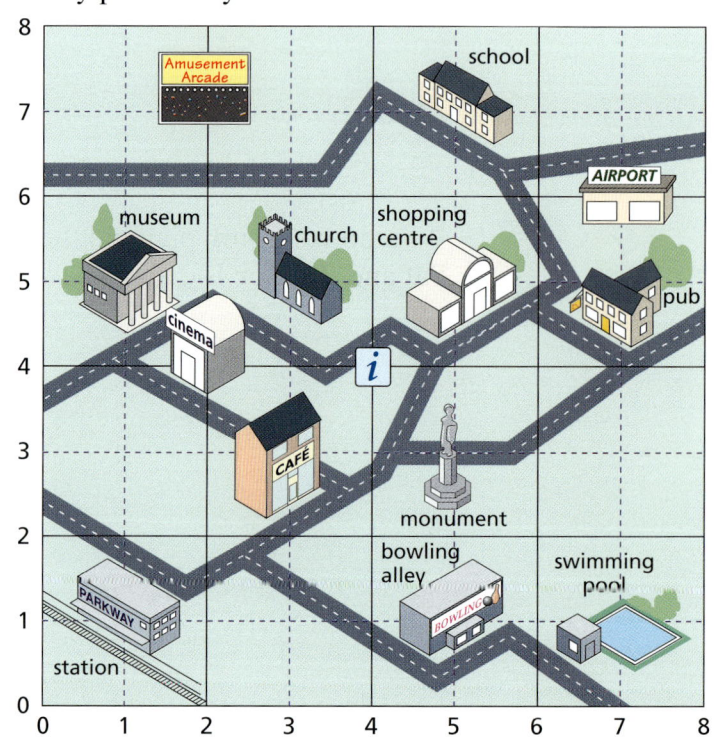

Write down the names of the places Pat and Kate visited, in this order.

a) Tourist Information Office   (4, 4)

b) _____ (1, 5)

c) _____ (7, 1)

d) _____ (3, 3)

e) _____ (5, 1)

17

> **Remember**
>
> We use pairs of numbers called **co-ordinates** to show where lines cross on a plan (**along the corridor**, **up the stairs**).

Write down the co-ordinates of the places Joe and Ella visited, in this order.

a) church – (3, 5)

b) airport – (,)

c) café – (,)

d) amusement arcade – (,)

e) shopping centre – (,)

f) Who do you think planned their day best – Pat and Kate **or** Joe and Ella?

18 What do you notice about the groups of places with these **co-ordinates**?

a) (1, 5) (3, 5) (5, 5) (7, 5)

b) (2, 7) (5, 7)

c) (7, 1) (7, 5) (7, 6)

UNIT 4 SHAPE AND SPACE

19 Pat, Kate, Joe and Ella went in different directions to get to different places.

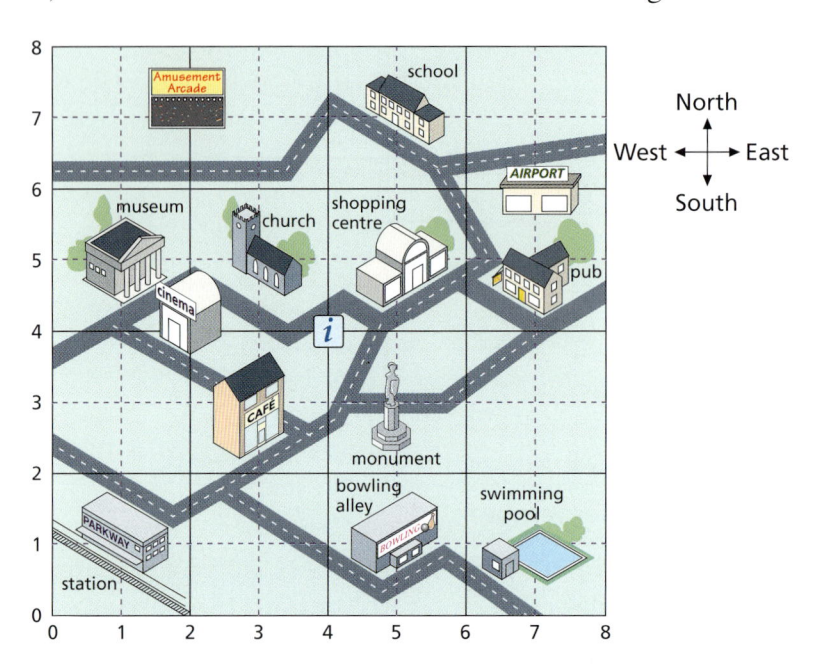

To go from the monument to the shopping centre, they went **North**.
We say the shopping centre is North of the monument.

a) To go from the pub to the airport, they went _____ .

   The airport is _____ of the pub.

b) To go from the monument to the bowling alley, they went _____ .

   The bowling alley is _____ of the monument.

c) To go from the café to the monument, they went _____ .

   The monument is _____ of the café.

d) To go from the church to the museum, they went _____ .

   The museum is _____ of the church.

e) Name two places North of the monument.

f) Name three places South of the school.

g) Name three places East of the museum.

h) Name two places West of the pool.

20 Try Worksheet Puzzle *Day out*.

Now try Unit 4 Test.

Review 4

1. What is the value of the circled ⓵?

   a) 2⓵   b) ⓵526   c) ⓵0050   d) 5⓵02

2. How many people does each **bar** stand for?
   Look carefully at each scale.

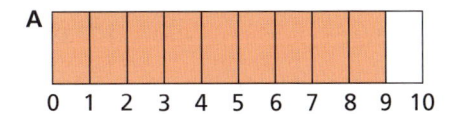

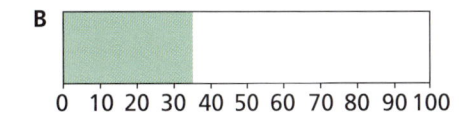

   A
   0 1 2 3 4 5 6 7 8 9 10

   B
   0 10 20 30 40 50 60 70 80 90 100

   a) Bar A shows ☐ people.   b) Bar B shows ☐ people.

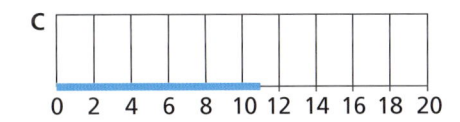

   C
   0 2 4 6 8 10 12 14 16 18 20

   c) Bar C shows ☐ people.

3. a) 3 + 7 + 8 = ☐   b) 3 + 9 + 7 = ☐

   c) 8 + 4 + 8 = ☐

4. a) 7 × 5 = ☐   b) 4 × 2 = ☐

   c) 8 × 10 = ☐   d) 3 × 5 = ☐

   e) ☐ × 2 = 18   f) ☐ × 10 = 50

   g) ☐ × 5 = 45

5. What value is the circled digit – **units** or **tenths**?

   a) 2.⓹   b) ⓷.6   c) 0.⓹

6. a) T U   b) T U   c) T U
        5 7   5 2   5 2
      – 1 2   –   8   – 2 8
      ─────   ─────   ─────

   d) T U   e) T U
        8 2   8 2
      –   7   – 3 7
      ─────   ─────

Review 4 • 43

UNIT 4 SHAPE AND SPACE

7 Look at the time on this clock.

Write the time if it was:

a) **1 hour** fast   b) **1 hour** slow

c) **½ hour** fast   d) **½ hour** slow

5 Number

Multiplication by 2, 3, 4, 5, 6 and 10

Unit 5 words

sign	answer	calculator
circle	digit	nought
thousand	group	zero
large	each	greater

Remember

Examples are shown in red.

means copy and complete.

You need
- a set of Unit 5 vocabulary Snap cards.

Play a game of Snap to help you learn the words.

Try the **word test** to get some points.

Remember

$2 + 2 + 2 + 2 + 2$
$= 5$ lots of 2
$= 5 \times 2 = 10$

1 You can find the answers to three of these sums in **two** ways.
   Find the three sums.
   Work them out both ways and find the answers.
   Which was the faster way?

a) $5 + 5 + 5 + 5 + 5 + 5 + 5 + 5 = \square$

b) $2 + 2 + 2 + 2 + 2 + 2 + 2 + 2 + 2 = \square$

c) $10 + 10 + 10 + 5 + 10 = \square$

d) $10 + 10 + 10 + 10 + 10 + 10 + 10 = \square$

e) $4 + 3 + 4 + 4 + 4 = \square$

UNIT 5 NUMBER

2 You need
- squared paper.

Look at the **rows of squares** to find the answers.

a) ☐☐☐ b) ☐☐☐
   ☐☐☐   ☐☐☐
   ☐☐☐   ☐☐☐
   ☐☐☐   ☐☐☐
              ☐☐☐

a) $4 \times 3 =$ ☐   b) $5 \times 3 =$ ☐

Continue drawing the pattern of squares for:

c) $6 \times 3 =$ ☐   d) $7 \times 3 =$ ☐

e) $8 \times 3 =$ ☐   f) $9 \times 3 =$ ☐

You need
- a calculator.

g) Use a calculator to check if your answers are right. Do them both ways: use the + and then the × sign.

3 Now copy and complete this ×3 table.

	×3
0	0
1	3
2	6
3	9
4	
5	
6	
7	
8	
9	
10	

Multiplication by 2, 3, 4, 5, 6 and 10 — 47

4 You need
   - squared paper or use Worksheet 1.

   Copy the grid below. **Circle** the numbers in your ×3 answers.

1	2	3	4	5	6	7	8	9	10
11	12	13	14	15	16	17	18	19	20
21	22	23	24	25	26	27	28	29	30

5 a) Write out all the missing ×3 **answers**.

   3 6 ☐ ☐ ☐ ☐ ☐ ☐ ☐ 30

   b) The answers are going up in ☐s.

   c) The next two numbers after 30 would be ☐ and ☐.

6 Try Worksheet 2 *Threes to 100*.

7 You buy tennis balls in packets of three.

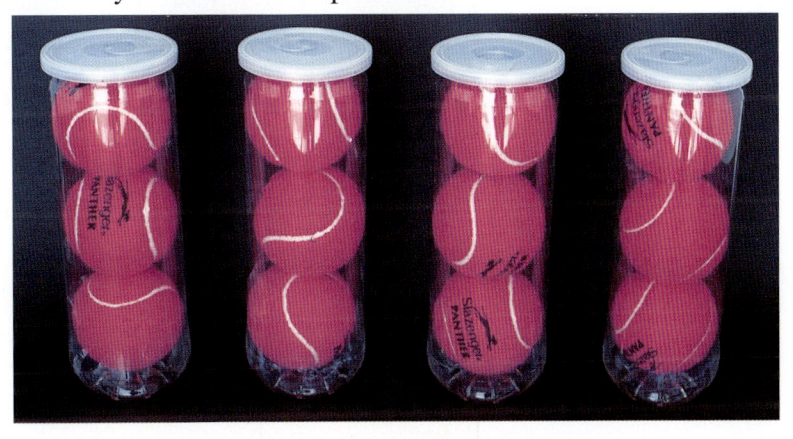

   a) You get ☐ tennis balls in 4 packets.
   b) You buy ☐ packets to get 12 tennis balls.
   c) You get ☐ tennis balls in 9 packets.
   d) You buy ☐ packets to get 27 tennis balls.
   e) You get ☐ tennis balls in 7 packets.
   f) You buy ☐ packets to get 21 tennis balls.

UNIT 5 NUMBER

8 Look at the pairs of dot patterns below.

Two rows of **three** make **six**.

Three rows of **two** make **six**.

> **Remember**
>
> Three rows of two and two rows of three give the **same** answer.

a) $2 \times 3 = \boxed{}$ b) $3 \times 2 = \boxed{}$

I can't remember the answer to 2×3.

Try 3×2 instead. That will give you the same answer.

If you need to, draw the dots to find the answers for:

c) $6 \times 3 = \boxed{}$ $3 \times 6 = \boxed{}$

d) $7 \times 3 = \boxed{}$ $3 \times 7 = \boxed{}$

e) $8 \times 3 = \boxed{}$ $3 \times 8 = \boxed{}$

f) $9 \times 3 = \boxed{}$ $3 \times 9 = \boxed{}$

g) $10 \times 3 = \boxed{}$ $3 \times 10 = \boxed{}$

9 You need
- a calculator.

Now try some **bigger** numbers.

a) 11×3 and 3×11 b) 25×3 and 3×25

c) 98×3 and 3×98 d) 152×3 and 3×152

What do you notice about each pair of answers?

Multiplication by 2, 3, 4, 5, 6 and 10 49

10 Look at the **rows of squares** to find the answers.

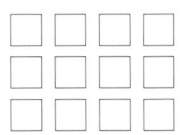

a) 3 × 4 = ☐   b) 5 × 4 = ☐

Continue drawing the pattern of squares for:

c) 6 × 4 = ☐   d) 7 × 4 = ☐

e) 8 × 4 = ☐   f) 9 × 4 = ☐

You need

- a calculator.

g) Use a calculator to check if your answers are right. Do them both ways: use the + and the × sign.

11 Now copy and complete this ×4 table.

	×4
0	0
1	4
2	8
3	12
4	
5	
6	
7	
8	
9	
10	

UNIT 5 NUMBER

12 You need
- squared paper or use Worksheet 1.

Copy the grid below. **Circle** the numbers in your ×**4** answers.

1	2	3	④	5	6	7	⑧	9	10
11	12	13	14	15	16	17	18	19	20
21	22	23	24	25	26	27	28	29	30
31	32	33	34	35	36	37	38	39	40

13 a) Write out all the missing ×**4 answers**.

4   8   ☐   ☐   ☐   ☐   ☐   ☐   40

> **Remember**
>
> Answers which are the same are called common.

b) The answers are going up in ☐s.

c) The next two numbers after 40 would be ☐ and ☐.

d) Look at the ×3 answers.
Are there any which are the **same** as ×4 answers?

14 Try Worksheet 3 *Common answers*.

15 You buy roller blade wheels in packets of four.

a) You get ☐ roller blade wheels in 5 packets.

b) You buy ☐ packets to get 20 roller blade wheels.

c) You get ☐ roller blade wheels in 8 packets.

d) You get ☐ roller blade wheels in 6 packets.

Multiplication by 2, 3, 4, 5, 6 and 10   51

e) You get ☐ roller blade wheels in 0 packets.

f) You buy ☐ packets to get 36 roller blade wheels.

g) You buy ☐ packets to get 28 roller blade wheels.

16 Look at the pairs of dot patterns below.

Five rows of **four** make **twenty**.

Four rows of **five** make **twenty**.

> **Remember**
>
> Five rows of four   and   four rows of five   give the **same** answer.

a) $5 \times 4 =$ ☐ $4 \times 5 =$ ☐

If you need to, draw the dots to find the answers for:

b) $6 \times 4 =$ ☐ $4 \times 6 =$ ☐

c) $7 \times 4 =$ ☐ $4 \times 7 =$ ☐

d) $8 \times 4 =$ ☐ $4 \times 8 =$ ☐

e) $9 \times 4 =$ ☐ $4 \times 9 =$ ☐

f) $10 \times 4 =$ ☐ $4 \times 10 =$ ☐

17 You need

- a calculator.

Now try some bigger numbers.

a) 12×4 and 4×12 b) 18×4 and 4×18

c) 78×4 and 4×78 d) 124×4 and 4×124

What do you notice about each pair of answers?

18 Karen's father has a farm. Karen goes around houses selling eggs.

She sells eggs in boxes of 6.

You can use a calculator to help you.
How many **eggs** would she sell if she sold the following boxes?

a) 1 box — 6 eggs

b) 2 boxes   c) 3 boxes   d) 4 boxes

e) 5 boxes   f) 6 boxes   g) 7 boxes

h) 8 boxes   i) 9 boxes   j) 10 boxes

19 You can use a calculator to help you.
How many boxes would she sell if she sold the following **eggs**?

a) 6 eggs — 1 box

b) 24 eggs   c) 30 eggs   d) 18 eggs

e) 12 eggs   f) 36 eggs   g) 54 eggs

h) 60 eggs   i) 42 eggs   j) 0 eggs

20 If you have learned your ×2, ×3, ×4, ×5, and ×10 tables you will already know some facts to help you with the ×6 table.
For example, you know that 6 × 2 = 12   so   2 × 6 = 12.

a) Which other facts have you already learned from other tables to help you with the ×6 table?

b) Which do you still need to learn?

Multiplication by 2, 3, 4, 5 and 10   53

21 Try Worksheet 4 *Number machines*.

22 Ann and Mike visit a sports shop.

sports socks (2 pairs in a pack) 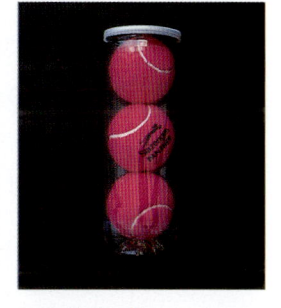   tennis balls

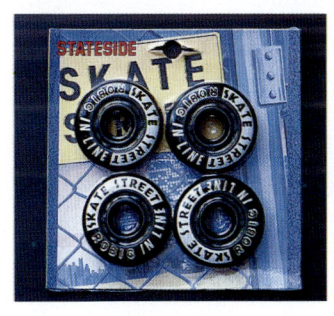

roller blade wheels    table tennis balls

Ann buys:
7 packs of socks   9 boxes of tennis balls
2 packs of roller blade wheels   5 boxes of table tennis balls
She has:

a) ☐ pairs of socks   b) ☐ tennis balls

c) ☐ roller blade wheels   d) ☐ table tennis balls

23 Ravi has: 10 pairs of socks   28 roller blade wheels
            54 table tennis balls   15 tennis balls
He has bought:

a) ☐ boxes of table tennis balls

b) ☐ packs of socks

c) ☐ packs of roller blade wheels

d) ☐ boxes of tennis balls

24 Try Worksheet 5 *Problem page*.

UNIT 5 NUMBER

25 Try Worksheet 6 *Fill the blanks*.

26 Try Worksheet Puzzle *Compare tables*.

27 You need
- Unit 5 Race against time cards Set 1 (×3), Set 2 (×4) and Set 3 (×6)
- your 'My maths record' sheet.

Race against time

1. Sort the race cards – this side up.
   (Do not mix up Set 1, Set 2 and Set 3.)
   Take the cards one at a time.
   Answer as quickly as you can.

   7×3

2. Look at the other side of the card for the answer.

   21

3. When you get all the answers correct, ask a friend to test you.

4. Now **Race against time**.
   Go for points!
   Ask your teacher to test and time you.

5. Now try Set 2 – this side up.

   6×4

6. Now try Set 3 – this side up.

   5×6

Remember
3 errors = 1 point   2 errors = 2 points
1 error = 3 points   0 errors = 5 points
Answer in 1 minute with 0 errors = 7 points

Now try Unit 5 Test.

Review 5

1. Write in pounds.

   a) 156p = £☐.☐☐   b) 102p = £☐.☐☐

2. Fill in the missing measures: **metres (m)   kilometres (km)   centimetres (cm) or millimetres (mm)**

   a) I measure a nail in _____ .

   b) I measure a journey in _____ .

   c) I measure a carpet in _____ .

   d) I measure my waist in _____ .

3. Pens are packed in **boxes of ten**.
   How many pens would you have if you bought:

   a) 6 boxes?   b) 9 boxes?   c) 7 boxes?   d) 10 boxes?

   How many **boxes** and how many **pens left over** if you had:

   e) 80 pens?   f) 87 pens?   g) 46 pens?   h) 100 pens?

4. Draw clocks and hands to show these times.

   a) twenty five to 7   b) twenty to 8   c) ten to 4   d) $\frac{1}{4}$ to 5

6 Shape and space
2D and 3D shapes

Unit 6 words

sliding pattern	turning pattern	symmetrical
direction	bar-line	guess
impossible	likely	unlikely
certain	half-way	sign

Remember

Examples are shown in red.

✏️ means copy and complete.

🏃 You need
- a set of Unit 6 vocabulary Snap cards.

🏃 Play a game of Snap to help you learn the words.

🏃 Try the **word test** to get some points.

Triangles

1 a) All the shapes below are called _____ .

X   Y   Z

b) They each have ☐ sides.

c) They each have ☐ angles.

2D and 3D shapes 57

You need
- a ruler to help you find out how many sides are **equal**.

d) X has ☐ equal sides.   e) Y has ☐ equal sides.

f) Z has ☐ equal sides.

2 You can use a right angle checker to find out if the angles in triangles are acute, obtuse or right-angled.

right angle   acute angle   obtuse angle
                less than a   more than a

Remember

Equal means **the same**.

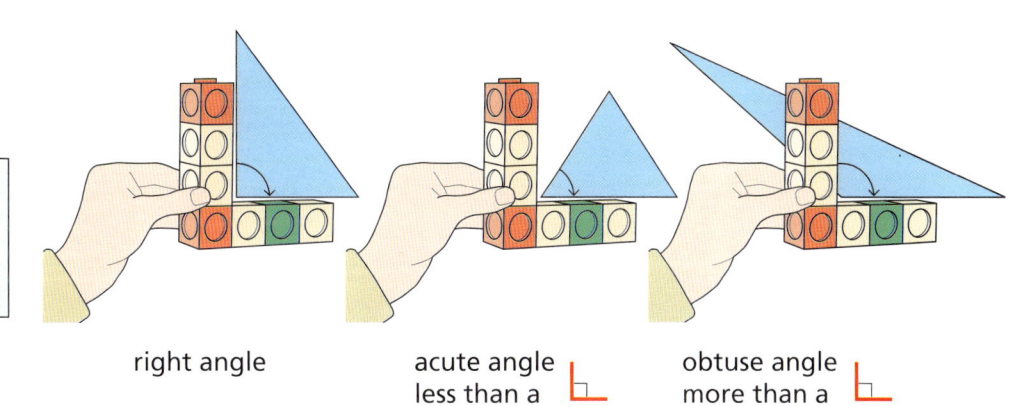

Or you could use a **set square** like this.

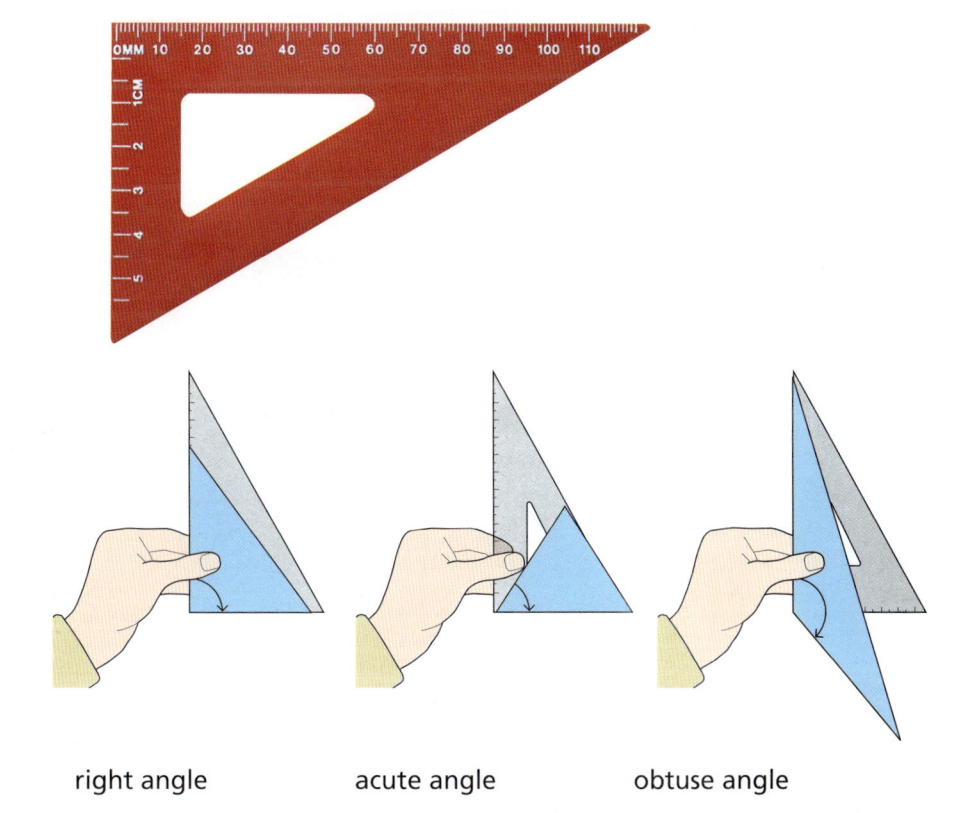

right angle   acute angle   obtuse angle

UNIT 6 SHAPE AND SPACE

You need
- a set square.

Look at the three angles in each of these triangles.

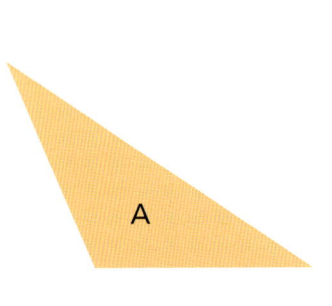

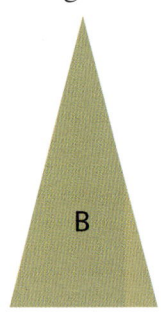

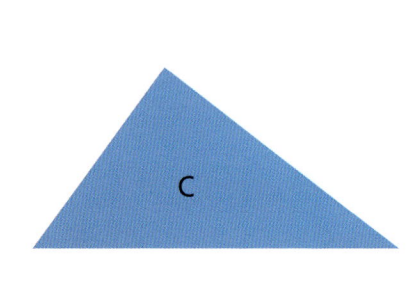

A   B   C

Use the set square to help you to copy and complete the table below.

Shape	Acute angles	Obtuse angles	Right angles
A	2	1	0
B			
C			

3 Try Worksheet 1 *Colour the angle*.

4 You need
- spotty paper
  or

  or

Answer **true** or **false**?
You can draw or make a triangle which has:

a) 3 acute angles

b) 2 obtuse and 1 acute angles

c) 2 acute and 1 obtuse angles   d) 3 obtuse angles

e) 1 right angle and 2 acute angles   f) 3 right angles

a) true

2D and 3D shapes 59

5 Sue and Jade use **right-angled triangles** to do some patchwork.

They cut around these to help make patterns like these.

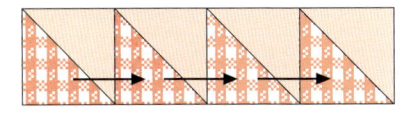

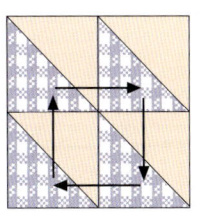

Try Worksheet 2 *Slide the shape*.

6 Jade puts 4 patterns together to make this cushion.

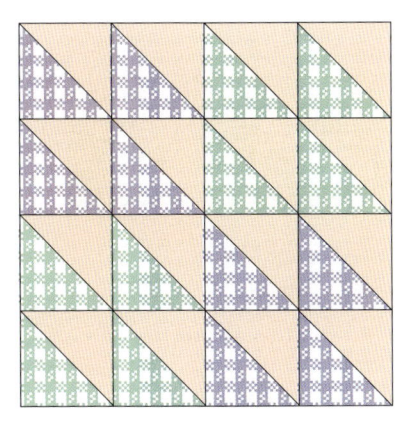

Try Worksheet 3 *Patchwork (1)*.

UNIT 6 SHAPE AND SPACE

7 Jade turns some of her patterns a half turn
from this   to   this.

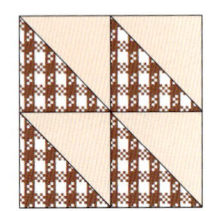

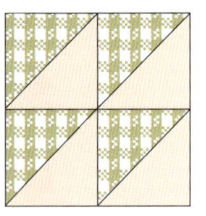

She puts 4 patterns together to make this cushion.

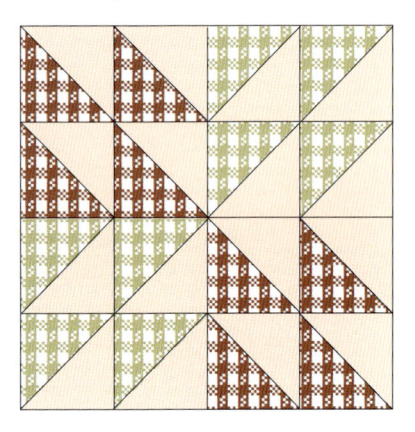

Try Worksheet 4 *Patchwork (2)*.

8 We can colour squares

to help make shapes like these.

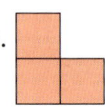

We can **slide** this shape to make a pattern.
Which of these patterns shows a **sliding pattern**:

pattern **A**   or   pattern **B**?

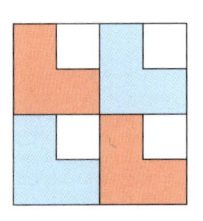

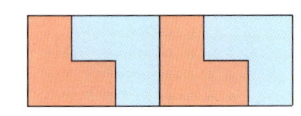

Pattern _____ shows the sliding pattern.

2D and 3D shapes   61

9 If we **turn** this shape **half** a turn and cut it out in a **different colour** it would look like this.

Which of these patterns shows a **turning** pattern –

pattern **A**   or   pattern **B**?

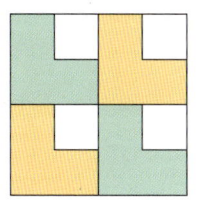

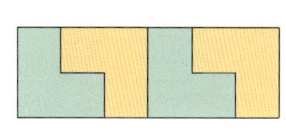

Pattern _____ shows a turning pattern.

10 Try Worksheet 5 *Turning shapes*.

11 Sue and Bob look at some patchwork to get ideas.

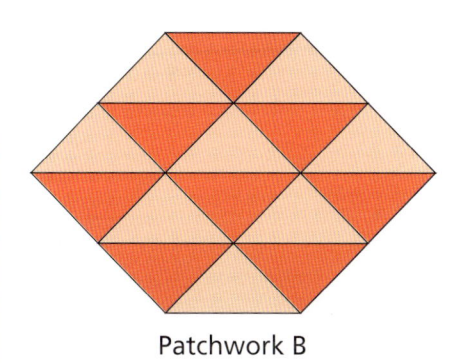

Patchwork A

Patchwork B

Sliding or turning?

a) Patchwork A shows a _____ pattern.

b) Look at Patchwork B. What patterns do you notice?

12 Try Worksheet Puzzle *Square up*.

UNIT 6 SHAPE AND SPACE

> **Remember**
>
> If something can be cut into two equal parts which are reflections of each other, we say it is **symmetrical**.

13 How many lines of symmetry can you see in this patchwork?

There are ☐ lines of symmetry.

14 We can fold and cut paper to make **symmetrical shapes**.

When we fold

and cut this paper,

it looks like this when we open it up.

You need
- squared paper.

a) Fold a square of paper and cut to make your own shape.

b) Draw the line of symmetry.

15 Try Worksheet 6 *Fold and cut*.

2D and 3D shapes   63

16 A paper square is folded two times like this.

A corner is cut off like this.

a) Which of these shapes do you think you will see when the paper is opened?

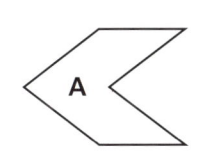

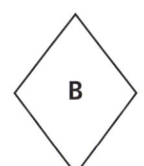

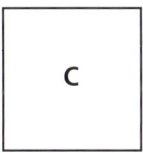

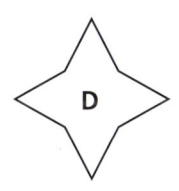

A   B   C   D

You will see shape _____ .

b) How many lines of symmetry do you think it will have?

It will have ☐ lines of symmetry.

17 You need
- multilink cubes
- a mirror.

Make this 3D shape with 5 multilink cubes.

UNIT 6 SHAPE AND SPACE

If the shape was reflected in a mirror it would look like this.

a) Try to copy the shape and reflect it in a mirror.

b) Make a **different** shape with 5 cubes.

c) Make the **mirror image** of the shape.
Use a mirror to see if you were right.

18 You need

- multilink cubes
- a mirror.

Look at this shape made with 8 multilink cubes.

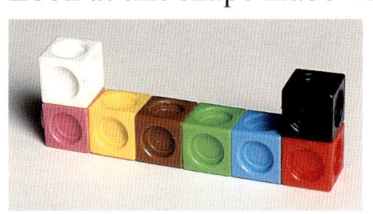

The shape below looks like the **same shape** made by using a mirror.

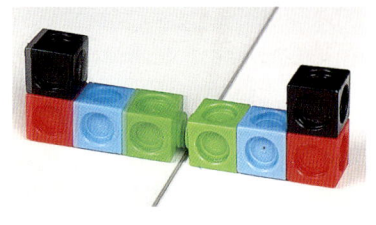

a) How many cubes would you need to use to make this shape **before** it was reflected in a mirror?

You would need to use ☐ cubes.

b) Make the shape and reflect it in a mirror to see if you were right.

19 Try Worksheet 7 *Mirror 3D*.

Now try Unit 6 Test.

Review 6

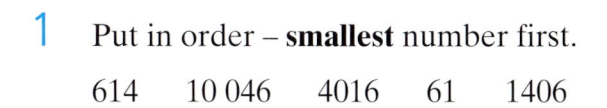

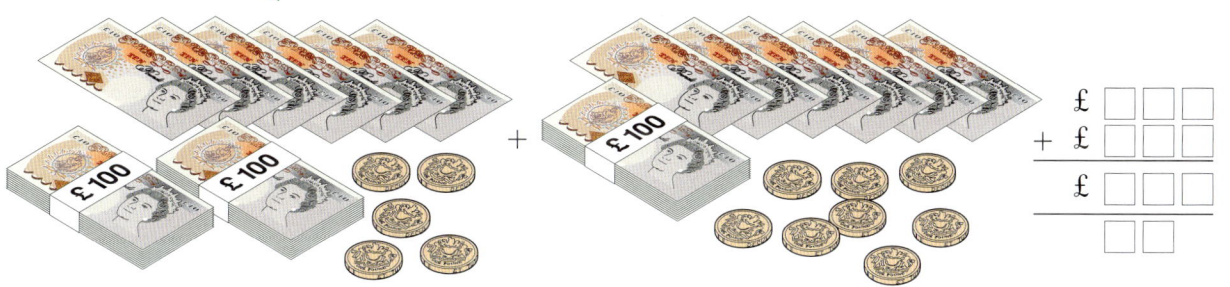

1. Put in order – **smallest** number first.

   614   10 046   4016   61   1406

2. How much money altogether?

3. Fill in the missing **decimal numbers**.

   a) 4.5   4.6   ☐.☐   4.8   ☐.☐   ☐.☐

   b) ☐.☐   1.9   ☐.☐   1.7   ☐.☐   1.5

4. Jack is 15 years old. Emma is 8 years old.

   a) Emma is ☐ years younger than Jack.

   b) Jack is ☐ years older than Emma.

   c) The **difference** in their ages is ☐ years.

5. Copy **only** the times which you could write as **p.m.** times.

   a) 08:30   20:30   3:30 in the afternoon   3:30 in the morning

   b) 16:20   4:50 in the afternoon   3:40 in the morning   03:15

   c) 7:10 in the evening   7:10 in the morning   19:15   07:15

7 Number

Decimal numbers to 2 decimal places

Unit 7 words

decimal point	whole number	hundredth
fraction	nought	pounds (£)
pence (p)	whole	decimal
amount	coins	guess

Remember

Examples are shown in red.

✎ means copy and complete.

You need
- a set of Unit 7 vocabulary Snap cards.

Play a game of Snap to help you learn the words.

Try the **word test** to get some points.

1 How much chocolate in **each** picture? Write as a **fraction** and as a **decimal**.

two whole bars → **2.3** ← **three tenths** $\frac{3}{10}$

↑
decimal point

$2\frac{3}{10}$ and 2.3

Decimal numbers to 2 decimal places • **67**

a)   b)

> **Remember**
>
> A **decimal point** separates the **whole numbers** from the **fractions**.

Addition

2 Tom and Sue eat chocolate.

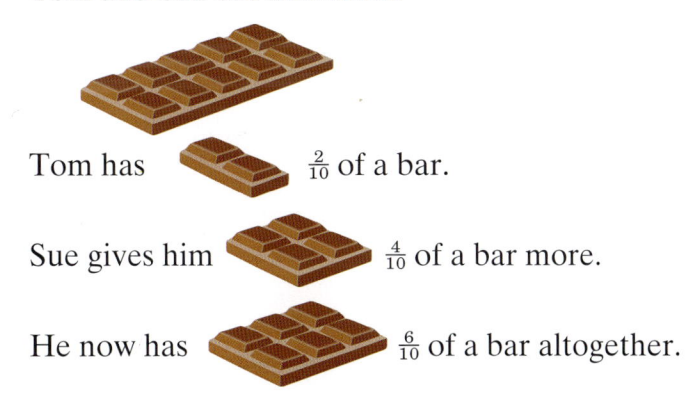

Tom has $\frac{2}{10}$ of a bar.

Sue gives him $\frac{4}{10}$ of a bar more.

He now has $\frac{6}{10}$ of a bar altogether.

We can write this as a fraction like this.

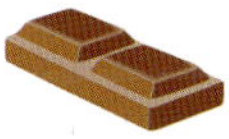

$\frac{2}{10} + \frac{4}{10} = \frac{6}{10}$

Add the following fractions.

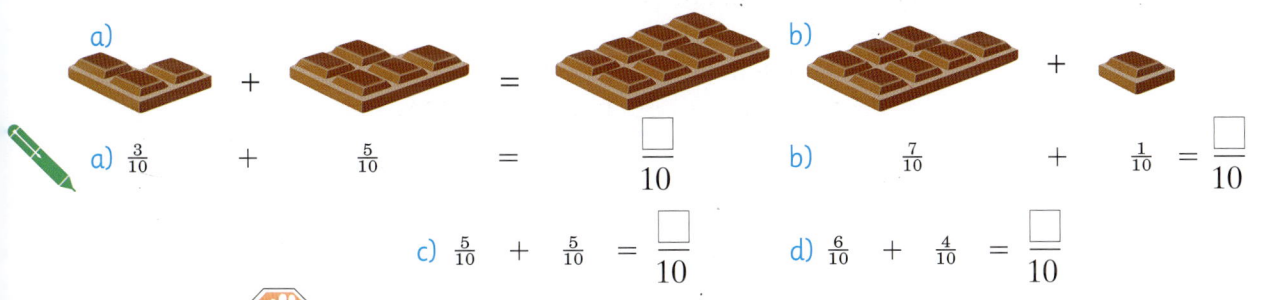

a)   b)

a) $\frac{3}{10} + \frac{5}{10} = \frac{\Box}{10}$ b) $\frac{7}{10} + \frac{1}{10} = \frac{\Box}{10}$

c) $\frac{5}{10} + \frac{5}{10} = \frac{\Box}{10}$ d) $\frac{6}{10} + \frac{4}{10} = \frac{\Box}{10}$

e) Can you think of another way to write the last two answers?

> **Remember**
>
> **10** tenths = **1** whole thing or **1** unit

68 UNIT 7 NUMBER

3 We can also write the sums as decimals like this.

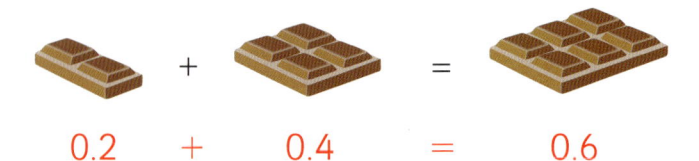

0.2 + 0.4 = 0.6

a)

a) 0.3 + 0.5 = ☐.☐
b) 0.2 + 0.6 = ☐.☐
c) 0.5 + 0.4 = ☐.☐

Remember

10 tenths = **1** whole thing (1.0)

d) 0.5 + 0.5 = ☐.☐
e) 0.6 + 0.4 = ☐.☐
f) 0.2 + 0.8 = ☐.☐

4 a) 0 . 6   b) 0 . 7   c) 0 . 8   d) 0 . 9
      +0 . 1   +0 . 1   +0 . 1   +0 . 1
      ─────   ─────   ─────   ─────
      ☐.☐   ☐.☐   ☐.☐   ☐.☐

5 Remeber that there are 10 chunks in one whole bar. How many **whole bars** could you make from:

a) 6 chunks?   b) 16 chunks?

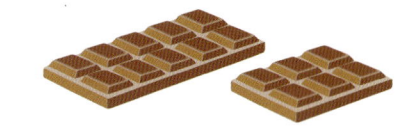

a) None   b) 1 bar (and 6 chunks)

c) 20 chunks?   d) 24 chunks?   e) 1 chunk?
f) 11 chunks?   g) 30 chunks?   h) 39 chunks?

Decimal numbers to 2 decimal places   69

6 How much chocolate would you have if you got:

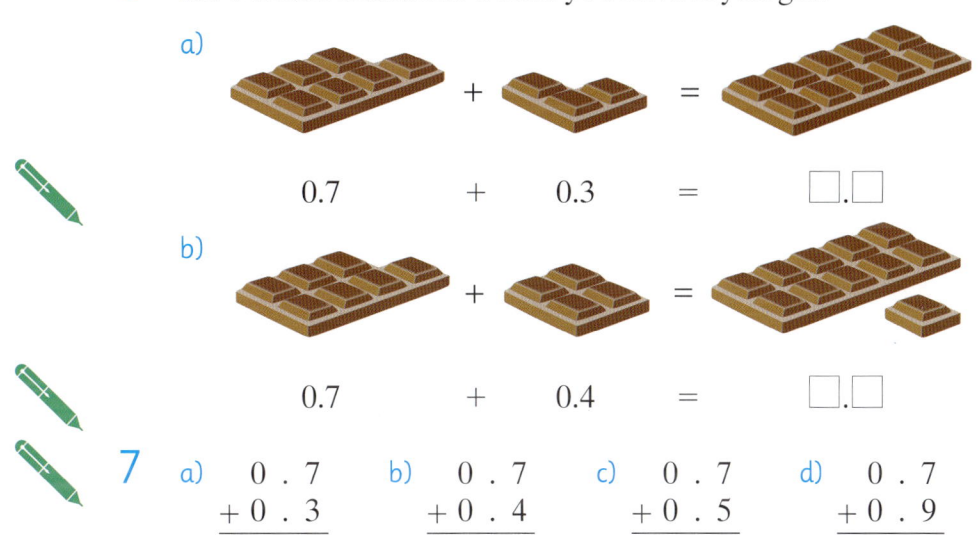

a) 0.7 + 0.3 = ☐.☐

b) 0.7 + 0.4 = ☐.☐

7 a) 0 . 7
   + 0 . 3
   ☐ . ☐

b) 0 . 7
   + 0 . 4
   ☐ . ☐

c) 0 . 7
   + 0 . 5
   ☐ . ☐

d) 0 . 7
   + 0 . 9
   ☐ . ☐

8 Try Worksheets 1 and 2 *Colour and add (1)* and *(2)*.

9 Look at the drawings to help you do these sums.

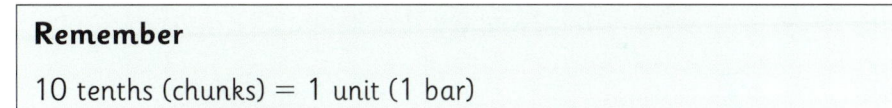

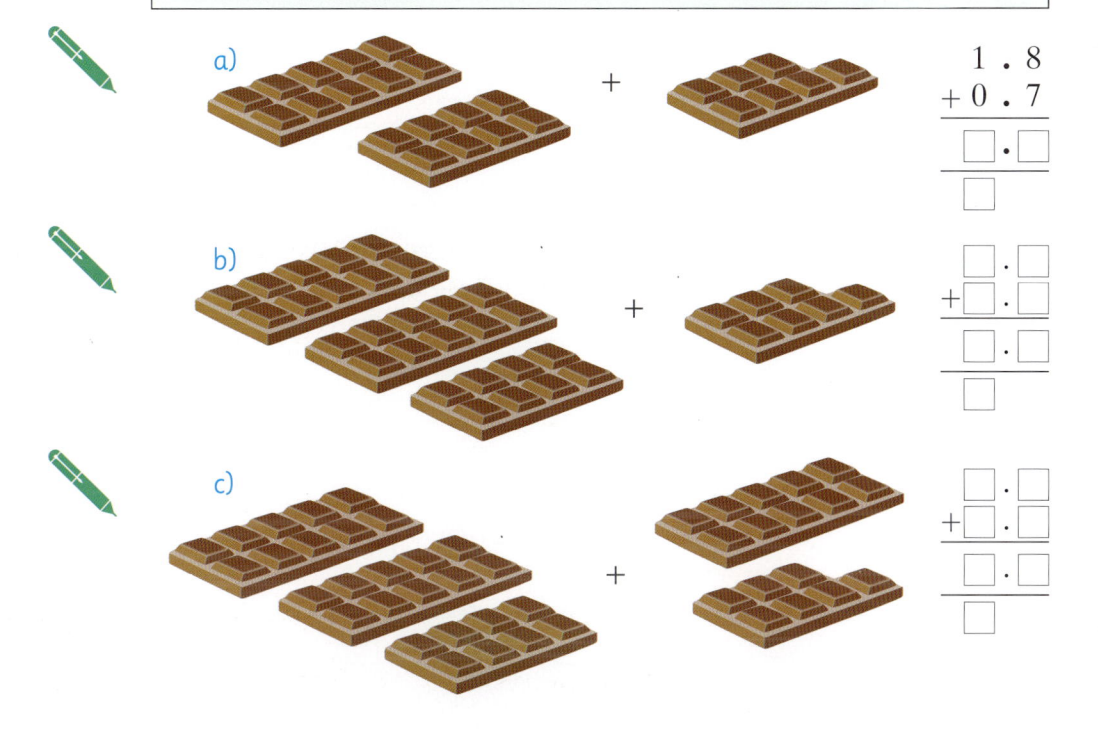

Remember

10 tenths (chunks) = 1 unit (1 bar)

a)   1 . 8
   + 0 . 7
   ☐ . ☐
   ☐

b)   ☐ . ☐
   + ☐ . ☐
   ☐ . ☐
   ☐

c)   ☐ . ☐
   + ☐ . ☐
   ☐ . ☐
   ☐

UNIT 7 NUMBER

Remember
There are 10 chunks in 1 whole bar.

Subtraction

10 Tom has [chocolate bar]. He eats [chocolate piece].

We can show how much he has left like this.

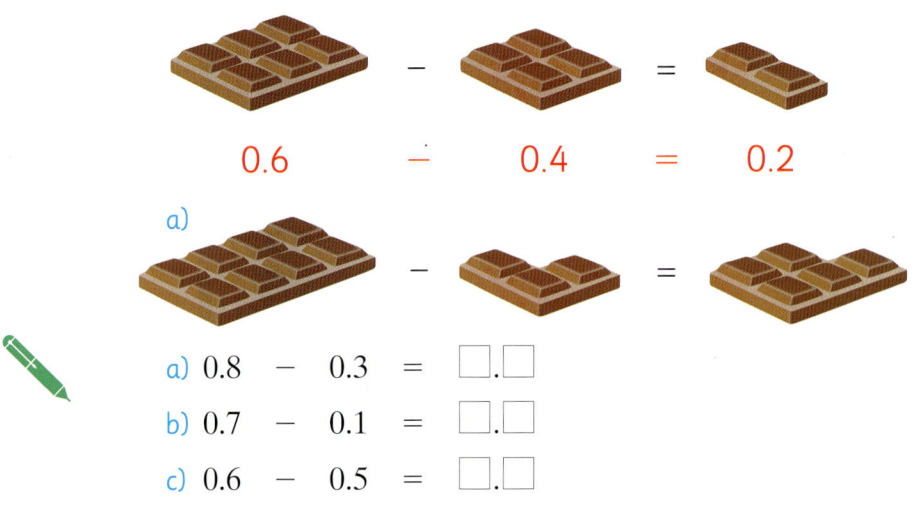

0.6   −   0.4   =   0.2

a)

a) 0.8 − 0.3 = ☐.☐
b) 0.7 − 0.1 = ☐.☐
c) 0.6 − 0.5 = ☐.☐

11 Now try Worksheet 3 *Chunks left (1)*.

12 Tom has a bar of chocolate.

Remember
1 whole (1.0) = 10 tenths

To eat three chunks he must break the bar.
We can set it out like this.

```
0 bars left ⟶    0   1
                 1̵.0  ⟵ 10 chunks
0 bars eaten ⟶ −0.3  ⟵ 3 chunks (tenths) eaten
0 bars left  ⟶  0.7  ⟵ 7 chunks (tenths) left
```

Set out your work to show when a bar was opened.

a) 1.0   b) 1.6   c) 1.0   d) 1.8
   −0.4   −0.4   −0.8   0.2
   ☐.☐   ☐.☐   ☐.☐   ☐.☐

Decimal numbers to 2 decimal places • **71**

13 How do you think you would set this out as a sum?

Tom has ⬚.

He eats ⬚.

How much chocolate does he have left?

14 Now try Worksheet 4 *Chunks left (2)*.

15 a) This is **1 whole** block of wood.

We can write it as **1 unit** or ☐.☐ .

Remember
If we divide something into **10 equal parts** each part is a **tenth** ($\frac{1}{10}$).

This is the block divided into **10 equal** pieces.

One tenth (**1** out of **10**) is coloured.

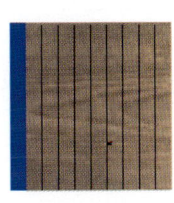

b) We can write this as $\frac{1}{10}$ or ☐.☐ .

c) There are $\frac{\square}{10}$ in the whole block.

16 There are ⬢ in ⬤

⬢ is 1/10 of ⬤

(one out of 10)

a) □/10 of £1

b) □/10 of £1

17 We write ⬢ as a decimal like this.

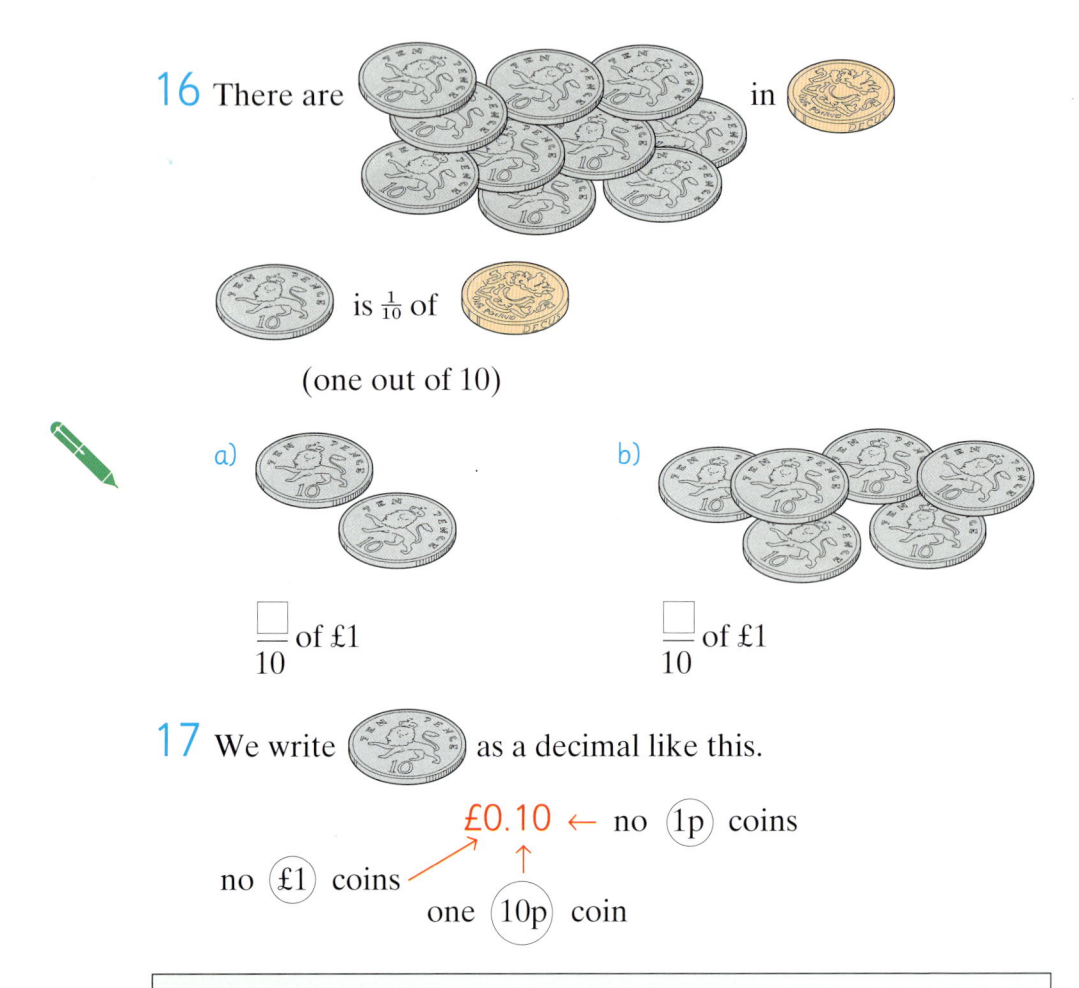

£0.10 ← no 1p coins
↑
no £1 coins
one 10p coin

Remember

When we use the decimal point and the £ sign to write money, we always have **2** numbers after the decimal point.

So when there are **no** 1p coins we put in a **0**.

Complete the following.

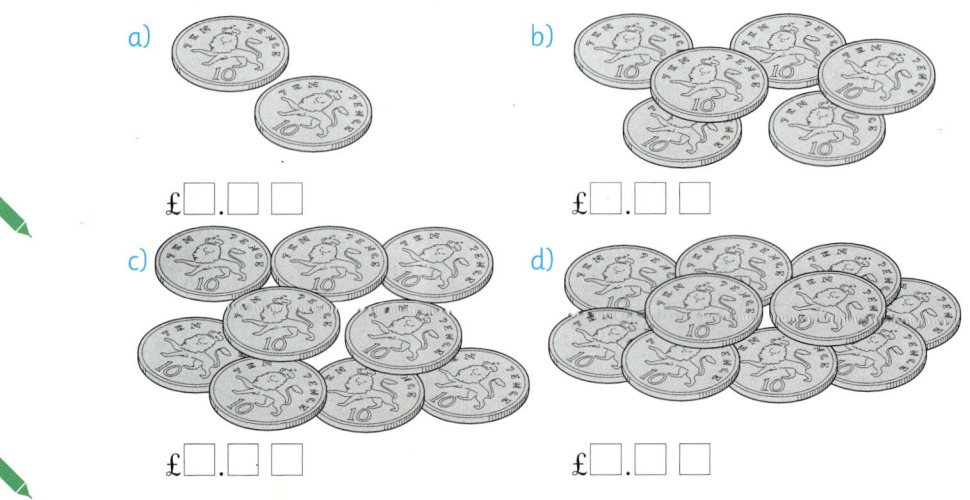

a) £□.□□

b) £□.□□

c) £□.□□

d) £□.□□

Decimal numbers to 2 decimal places • 73

18 This block is divided into **100 equal** pieces.

> **Remember**
>
> If we divide something into **100 equal parts** each part is a **hundredth** ($\frac{1}{100}$).

One **hundredth** (**1** out of **100**) is coloured.

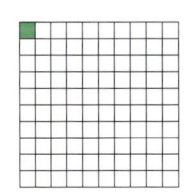

We write **one hundredth** like this as a fraction → $\frac{1}{100}$

There are $\frac{\Box}{100}$ in 1 whole block.

19 We write **one hundredth** like this as a decimal.

no units → 0.01 ← **one** hundredth
↑
no tenths

We say: *Nought point nought one.*

Write each green part as a **fraction** and as a **decimal** of the whole square.

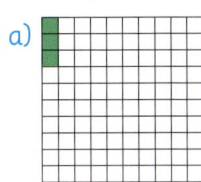

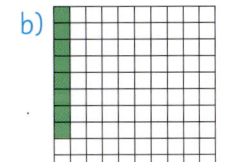

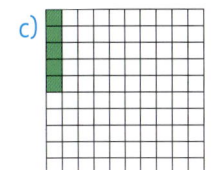

a)   b)   c)

a) $\frac{3}{100}$ or 0.03

UNIT 7 NUMBER

20 Try Worksheet 5 *Colour a hundredth*.

21 There are **100** 🪙 in 🪙

a)  🪙 is $\frac{1}{100}$ of 🪙

(one out of 100)

a) 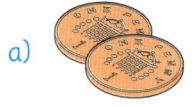 🪙🪙 $\frac{\square}{100}$ of £1

b) 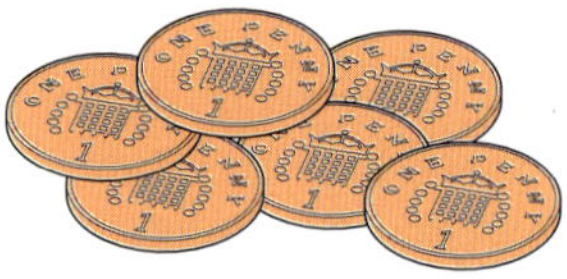 🪙🪙🪙🪙🪙 $\frac{\square}{100}$ of £1

22 We write 🪙 as **no** pounds → **£0.01** ← **one** pence (**1p**)

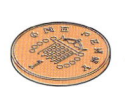

↑

no ten pence (**no 10p**)

Complete the following.

a) 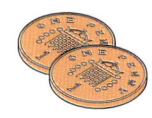 🪙🪙   £☐.☐☐

b)  🪙🪙🪙🪙🪙   £☐.☐☐

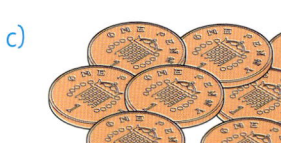

c) 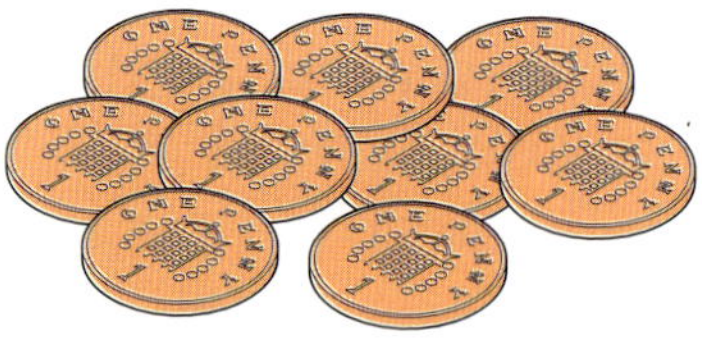 🪙🪙🪙🪙🪙🪙🪙   £☐.☐☐

d) 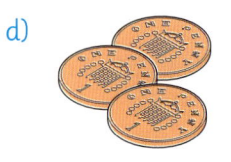 🪙🪙🪙   £☐.☐☐

Decimal numbers to 2 decimal places • 75

23 Write the blue parts as decimals.

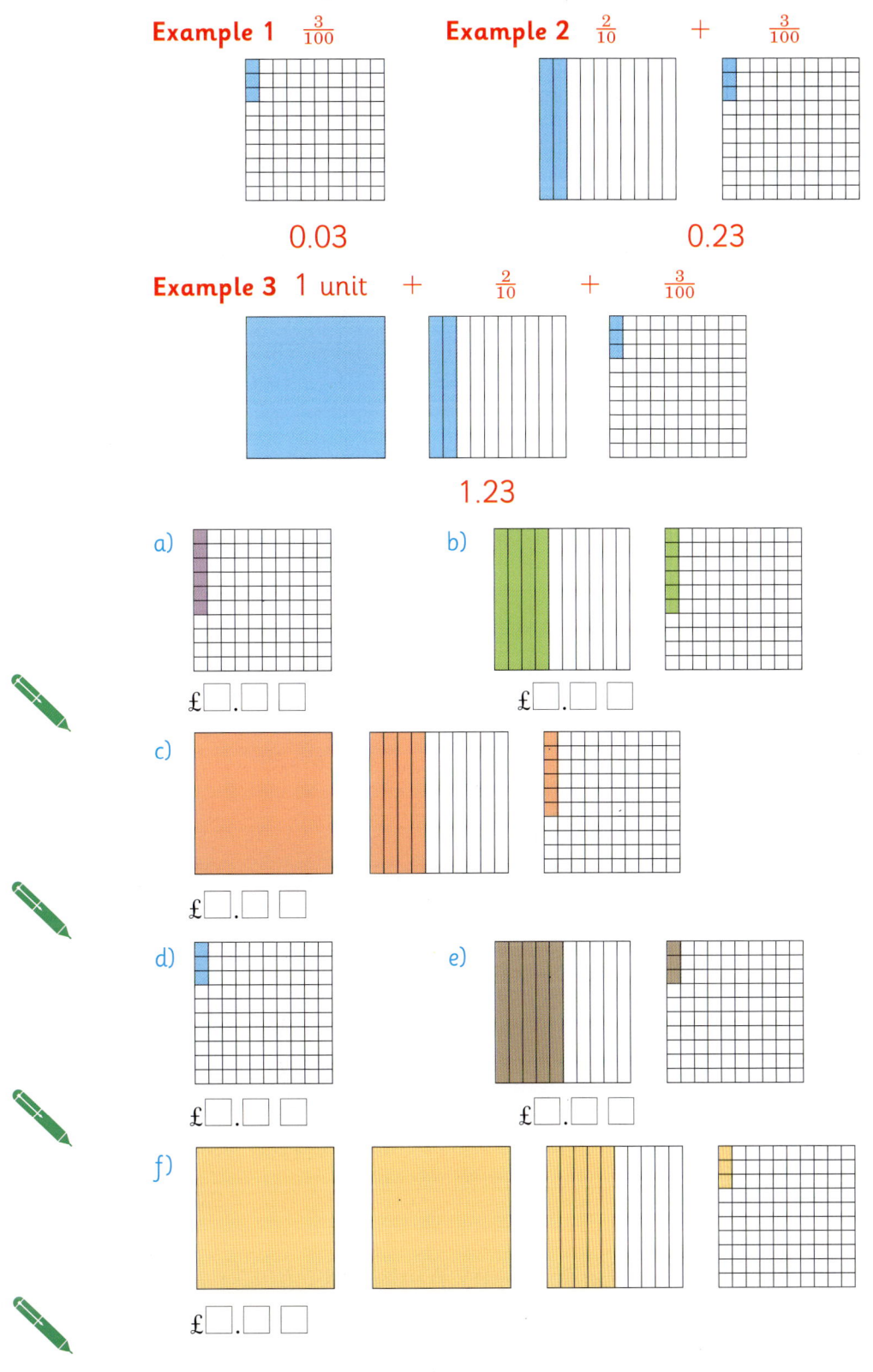

Example 1 $\frac{3}{100}$

0.03

Example 2 $\frac{2}{10}$ + $\frac{3}{100}$

0.23

Example 3 1 unit + $\frac{2}{10}$ + $\frac{3}{100}$

1.23

a) £☐.☐☐

b) £☐.☐☐

c) £☐.☐☐

d) £☐.☐☐

e) £☐.☐☐

f) £☐.☐☐

UNIT 7 NUMBER

24 Write these amounts of money as **decimals**.

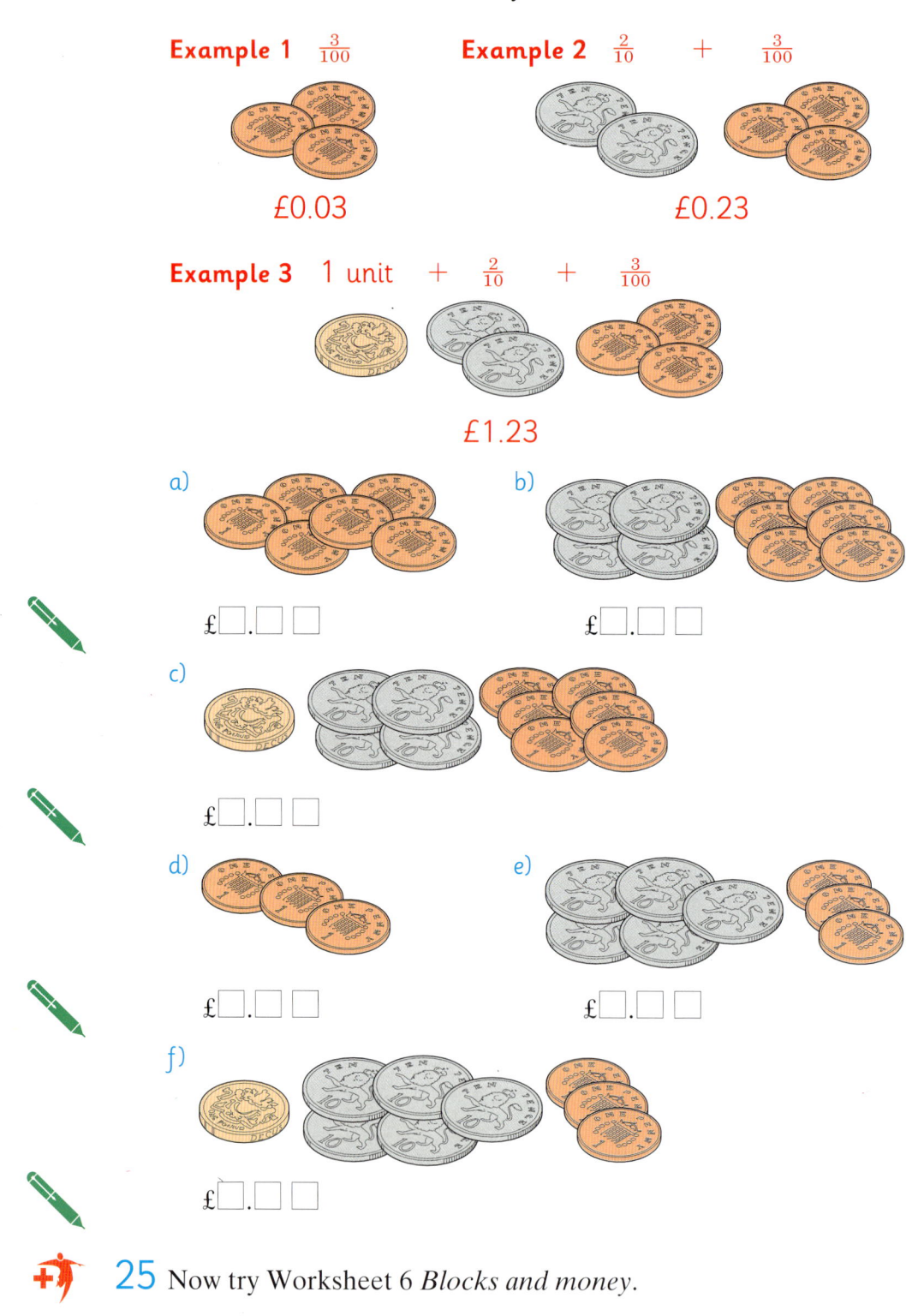

Example 1 $\frac{3}{100}$

£0.03

Example 2 $\frac{2}{10}$ + $\frac{3}{100}$

£0.23

Example 3 1 unit + $\frac{2}{10}$ + $\frac{3}{100}$

£1.23

a) £☐.☐☐

b) £☐.☐☐

c) £☐.☐☐

d) £☐.☐☐

e) £☐.☐☐

f) £☐.☐☐

25 Now try Worksheet 6 *Blocks and money*.

Decimal numbers to 2 decimal places • 77

26 You need
- a calculator.

Three people wanted to add up this weekly bill.

```
Lunches      £6.25
Magazines      25p
Bus fares    £2.80
```

These are the answers they got.

I got £34.05   *I got £9.30*   *I got £11.55*

Rose   Mo   Jake

a) Who do you think got the right answer?
Use your calculator to check.

Remember

When you enter an amount of money into a calculator, always enter it as a decimal.

b) What do you think the other two did wrong?

c) Can you think of a way to get a rough idea of the answer without using a calculator?

27 Which is the bigger amount:

a) £0.03 or £0.30? b) £0.05 or £0.50?

c) £1.70 or £1.07? d) £8.45 or £8.54?

UNIT 7 NUMBER

28 You need:
- Unit 7 Race against time cards
- your 'My maths record' sheet.

Race against time

1. Sort the race cards – this side up.
   Take the cards one at a time.
   Answer as quickly as you can.

2. Look at the other side of the card for the answer.

3. When you get all the answers correct, ask a friend to test you.

4. Now **Race against time**.
   Go for points!
   Ask your teacher to test and time you.

| 2.4 ⑦ |

| hundredths |

Remember
3 errors = 1 point   2 errors = 2 points
1 error = 3 points   0 errors = 5 points
Answer in 1 minute with 0 errors = 7 points

Now try Unit 7 Test.

Review 7

1. Draw a grid like this.

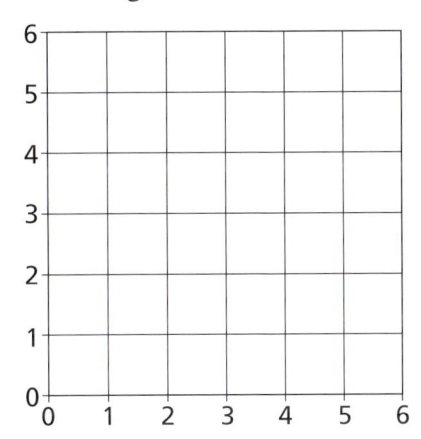

   Mark these points on it.
   (2, 0), (1, 2), (2, 4), (4, 4), (5, 2), (4, 0), (2, 0)

   Join up the dots.
   What shape have you drawn?

   I have drawn a _____ .

2. a) $9 \times 3 = \square$ b) $6 \times 4 = \square$ c) $4 \times 0 = \square$
   d) $7 \times 4 = \square$ e) $\square \times 10 = 0$ f) $\square \times 3 = 24$
   g) $\square \times 4 = 32$

3. Write down **all** the **pairs** which are **equal**.

1000 ml	1½ litres
½ litre	500 ml
1500 ml	1 litre

500 g	1½ kg
1 kg	½ kg
1500 g	1000 g

   1500 ml and 1½ litres

4. Find a half ($\frac{1}{2}$), and a quarter ($\frac{1}{4}$) and a tenth ($\frac{1}{10}$) of these buttons.

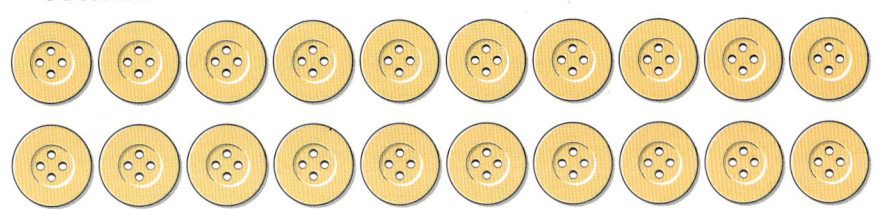

8 Measures

Length and weight

Unit 8 words

exact	**weigh**	weight
length	centimetre (cm)	millimetre (mm)
measure	metre (m)	kilometre (km)
kilogram (kg)	scale	order

Remember

Examples are shown in red.

✎ means copy and complete.

You need
- a set of Unit 8 vocabulary Snap cards.

Play a game of Snap to help you learn the words.

Try the **word test** to get some points.

A Length

1 You need
   - a 30 cm ruler.

   Look at this part of your ruler.

   0cm 1 2 3 4 5

   We write centimetre as _____ for short.

Length and weight 81

2 Measure the length of the hem A and hem B.

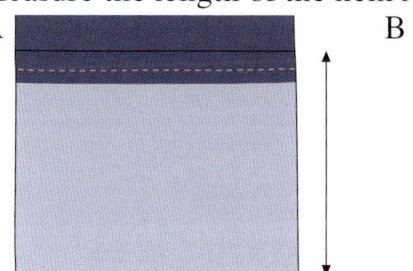

A B

a) Hem A measures ☐ cm.   b) Hem B measures ☐ cm.

Now try measuring hem C.

C

c) Hem C measures **about** ☐ cm.

d) Which hems were the easiest to measure?

3 When things we measure are **not an exact** number of centimetres, we can use **decimals** to measure them **more accurately**.
If we look at **2 cm – 3 cm** on a ruler through a magnifying glass, we see that it is divided into **10** equal parts.

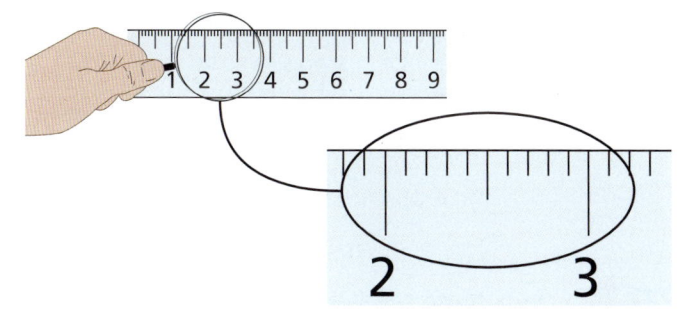

Each part is **one tenth** of a centimetre.

a) We can write $\frac{1}{10}$ cm as a decimal, ☐.☐ cm.

b) We can write $2\frac{1}{10}$ cm as a decimal, ☐.☐ cm.

UNIT 8 MEASURES

c) Write down the missing decimals in order – **smallest** first.

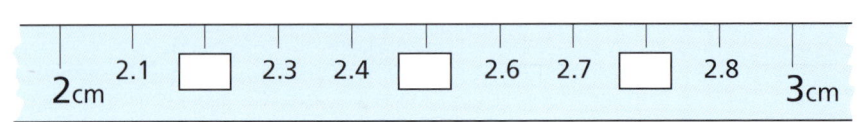

2cm 2.1 ☐ 2.3 2.4 ☐ 2.6 2.7 ☐ 2.8 3cm

Remember

You can use **decimals** to measure things more accurately.

4   This hem does **not** measure an **exact number** of cm.

This hem is **roughly 2 cm**.
If we measure it more **accurately**, it is $2\frac{3}{10}$ cm or 2.3 cm.

What do each of these hems measure?

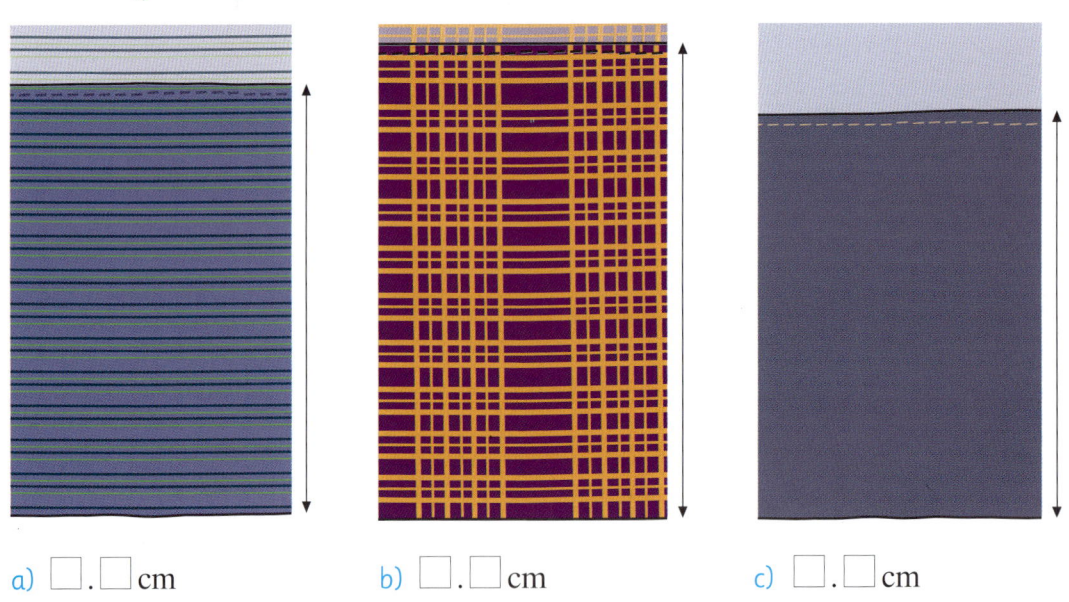

a) ☐.☐ cm   b) ☐.☐ cm   c) ☐.☐ cm

5   Now try Worksheet 1 *Riddle lines*.

Length and weight 83

6 From 8.7 cm move on 0.5 cm.

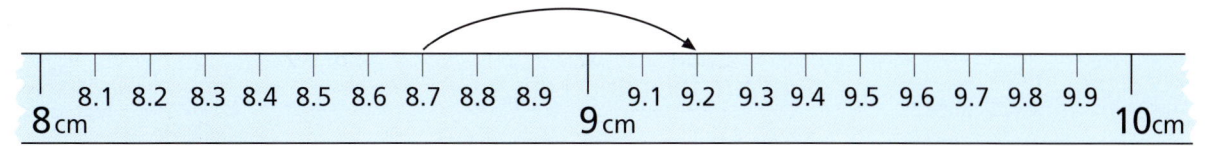

8 cm 8.1 8.2 8.3 8.4 8.5 8.6 8.7 8.8 8.9 9 cm 9.1 9.2 9.3 9.4 9.5 9.6 9.7 9.8 9.9 10 cm

a) 8.7 cm + 0.5 cm = ☐.☐ cm

b) 8 . 7 cm
   +0 . 5 cm
   ─────────
    ☐.☐ cm

7 Now try Worksheets 2 and 3 *Move on in decimals (1)* and *(2)*.

8 If the hems drawn in **Question 4** were **too short**, what length would they be if we made them **0.8 cm longer**?

2.3 cm

3.1 cm

2.3 cm + 0.8 cm = 3.1 cm   or   2 . 3
                                     +0 . 8
                                     ──────
                                      3 . 1
                                        1

9 We can also use **millimetres** to measure things more **accurately**.

Look at this part of your ruler.

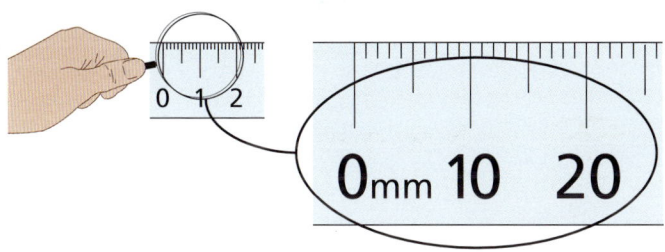

0 mm 10 20

We write millimetres as _____ for short.

UNIT 8 MEASURES

Remember

Look carefully to see if you must measure in **cm** or **mm**.

10 Draw these pairs of lines **exactly underneath** each other.

Draw lines which are:

a) 10 mm long and 1 cm long.

b) 30 mm long and 3 cm long.

c) 50 mm long and 5 cm long.

d) 100 mm long and 10 cm long.

e) 150 mm long and 15 cm long.

f) 200 mm long and 20 cm long.

g) What do you notice about each **pair of lines**?

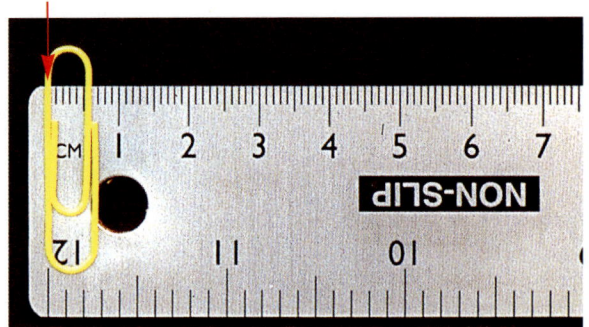

11 This paper clip is 6 millimetres (mm) wide.
Remember to measure from here.

Measure these screws in **millimetres** – you can write **mm** for short.

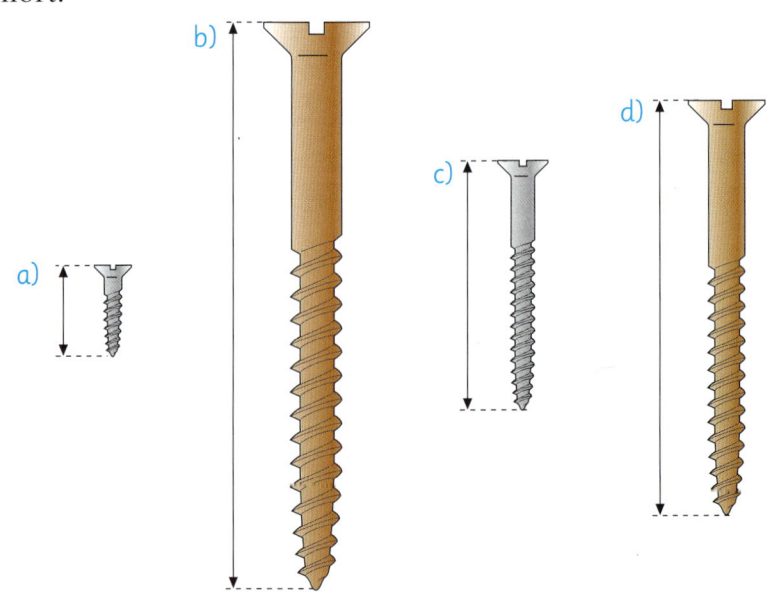

Length and weight

12 You measured the hems **accurately** in **Question 4** in **decimal cm**.
Now measure them in **mm**.

> **Remember**
>
> You can use **mm** to measure things more accurately.

What do you notice about these answers and the answers to **Question 4**?

13 A tile has fallen off the wall.
Measure the tiles below to find the missing one.

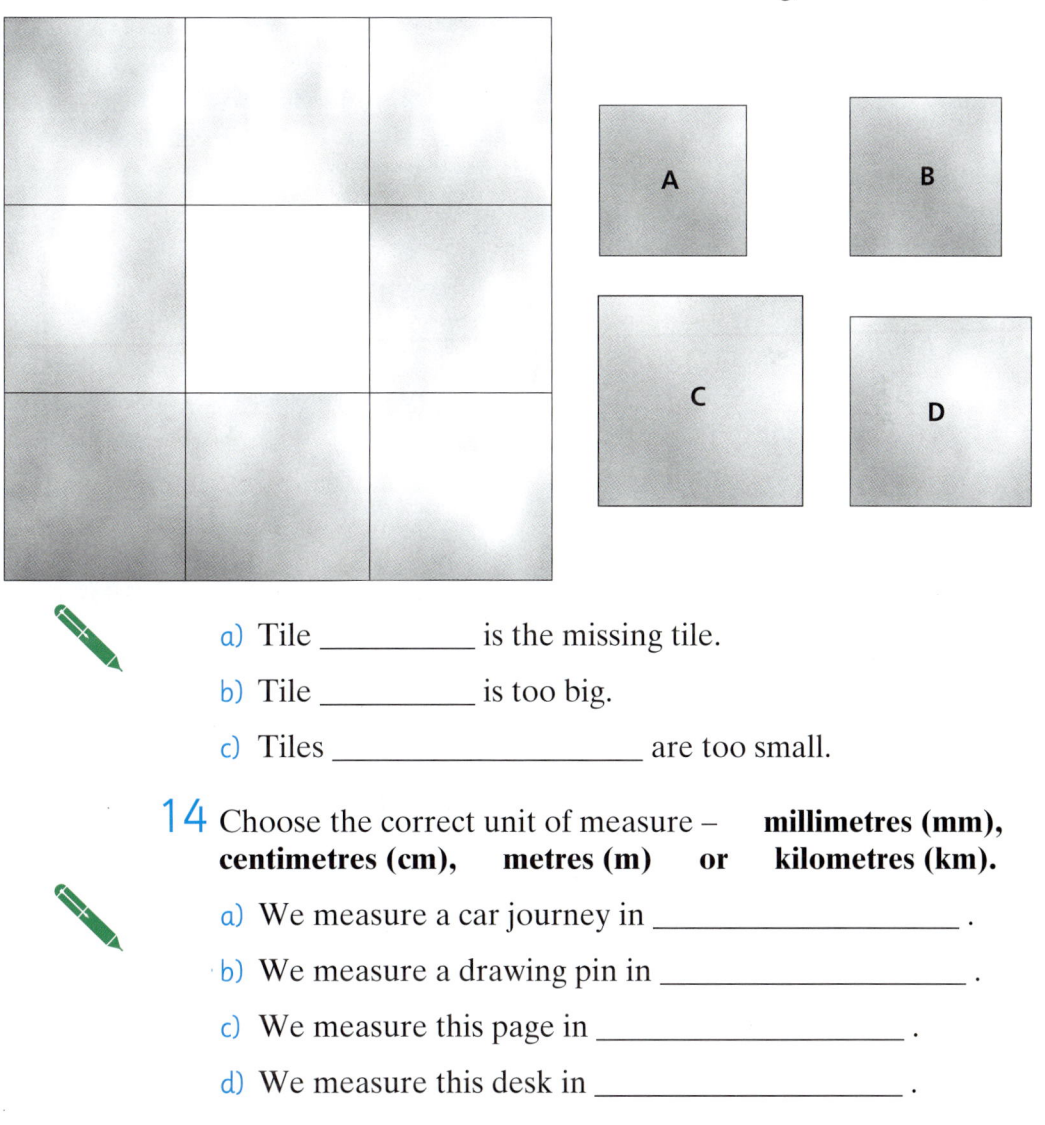

a) Tile _____ is the missing tile.

b) Tile _____ is too big.

c) Tiles _____ are too small.

14 Choose the correct unit of measure – **millimetres (mm), centimetres (cm), metres (m) or kilometres (km).**

a) We measure a car journey in _____ .

b) We measure a drawing pin in _____ .

c) We measure this page in _____ .

d) We measure this desk in _____ .

B Weight

You may use a calculator to help you.

1 There is a **1 kg** weight on **one** side of the scale each time. Add the weights on the **other** side of the scale.

Are they **more than**, **less than** or **equal to** one kilogram?

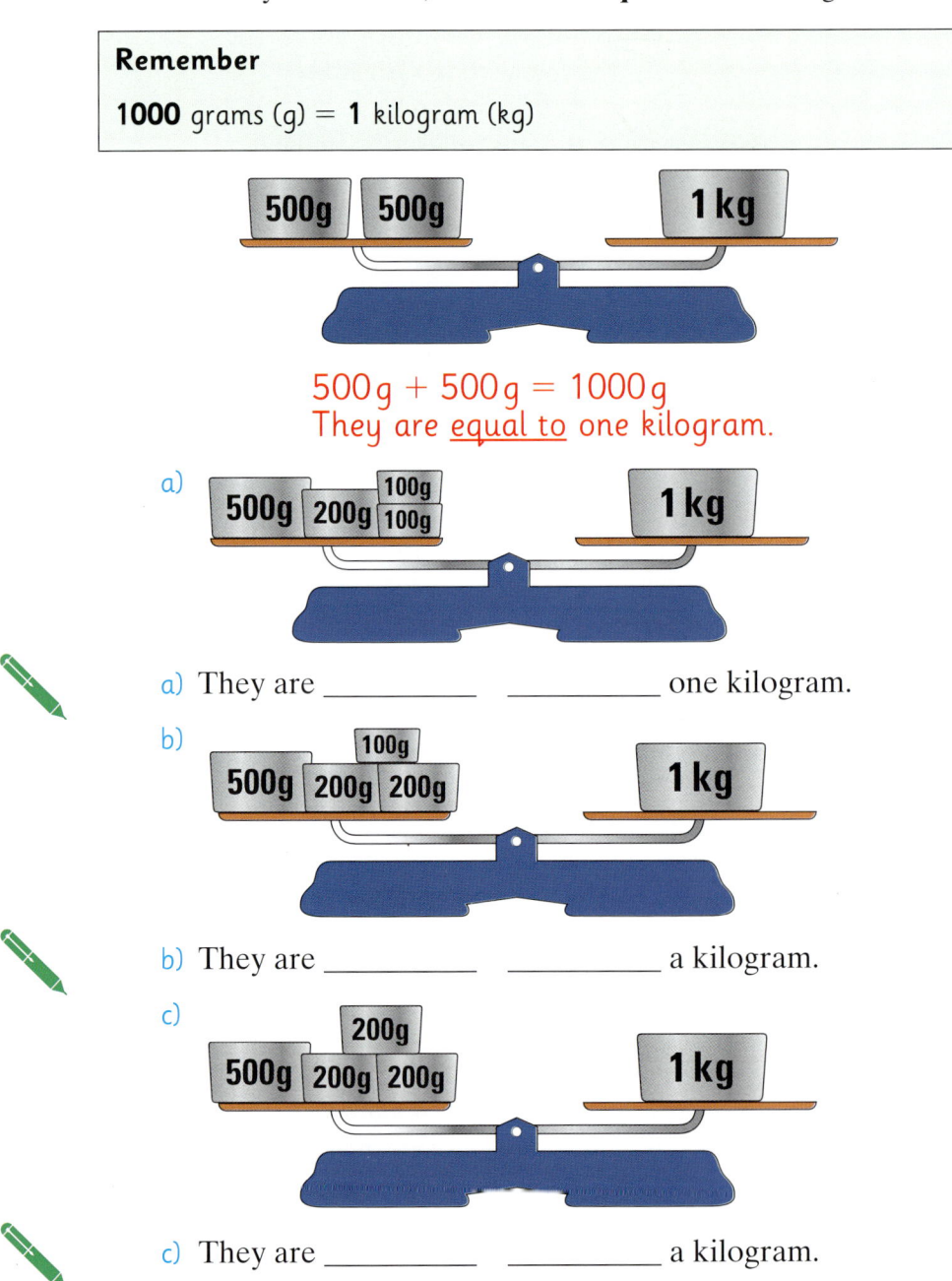

> **Remember**
> **1000** grams (g) = **1** kilogram (kg)

500 g + 500 g = 1000 g
They are equal to one kilogram.

a) They are _____ _____ one kilogram.

b) They are _____ _____ a kilogram.

c) They are _____ _____ a kilogram.

Length and weight **87**

2 The scale below measures in **kilograms** and **grams**.

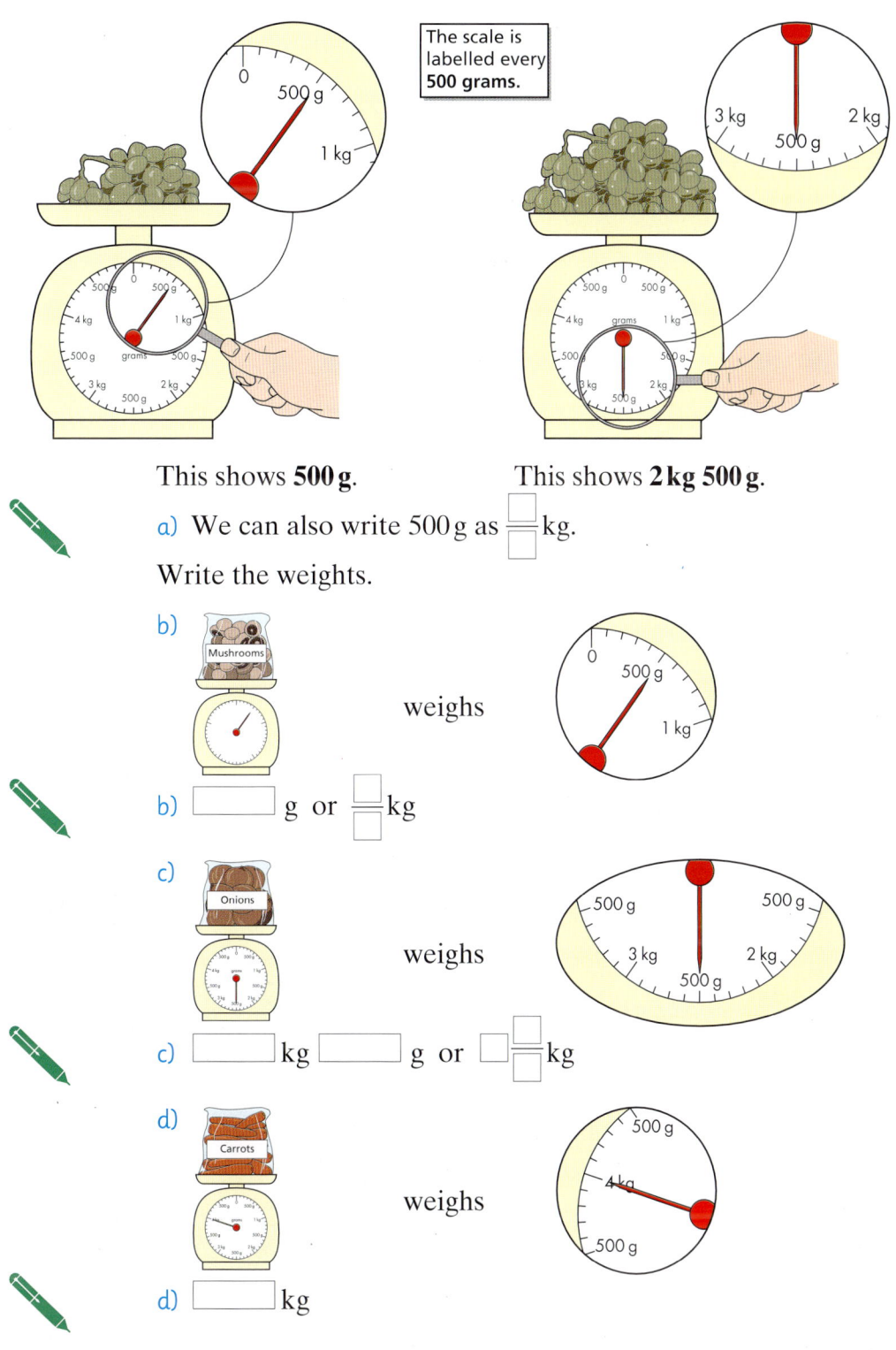

The scale is labelled every **500 grams**.

This shows **500 g**.   This shows **2 kg 500 g**.

a) We can also write 500 g as ▢/▢ kg.

Write the weights.

b) Mushrooms weighs

b) ▢ g or ▢/▢ kg

c) Onions weighs

c) ▢ kg ▢ g or ▢/▢ kg

d) Carrots weighs

d) ▢ kg

UNIT 8 MEASURES

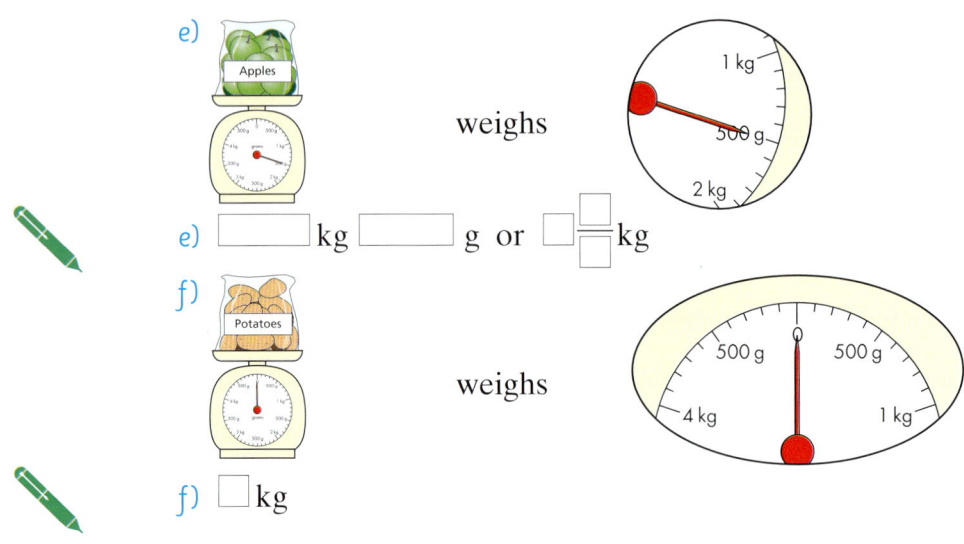

e) Apples weighs [shows 750 g / between 500 g and 1 kg]

e) ▢ kg ▢ g or ▢/▢ kg

f) Potatoes weighs [shows 1 kg]

f) ▢ kg

3 Some extra grapes in a bag are added to the grapes on the scales below.

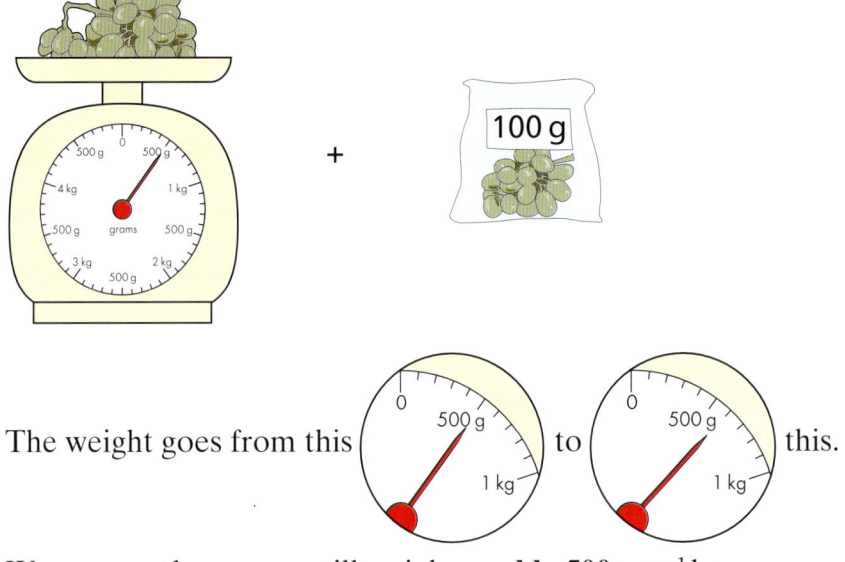

[scale showing grapes] + 100 g [bag of grapes]

The weight goes from this [scale] to [scale] this.

We can say the grapes still weigh **roughly 500 g** or $\frac{1}{2}$ kg.
What are these weights **roughly** to the nearest 500 g or $\frac{1}{2}$ kg?

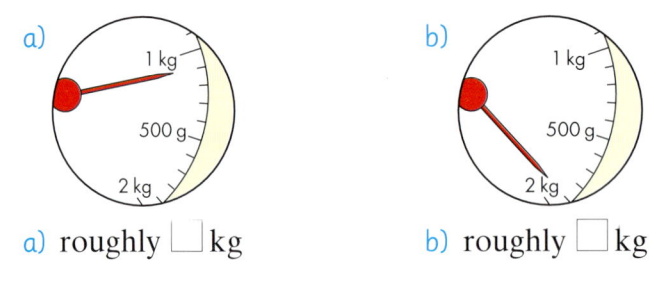

a) [scale]   b) [scale]

a) roughly ▢ kg   b) roughly ▢ kg

Length and weight   89

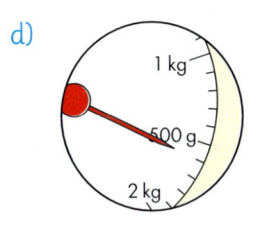

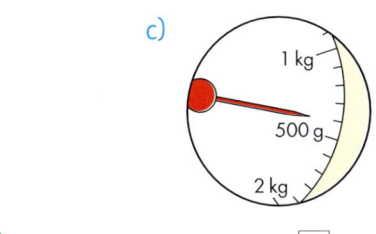

c) roughly ☐ kg ☐ g

d) roughly ☐ kg ☐ g

4 Some scales are labelled every 250 g.
This weigh scale shows **1 kg 750 g**.

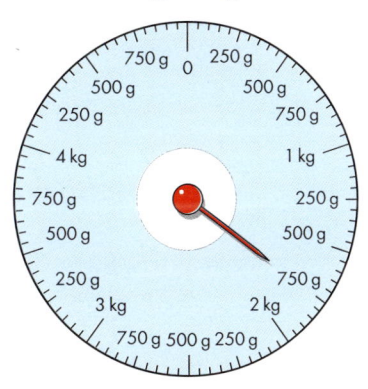

Write down the weights shown on the scales below.

a) ☐ kg ☐ g

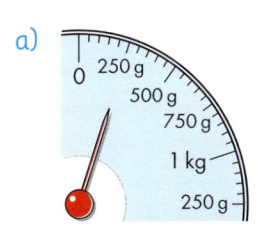

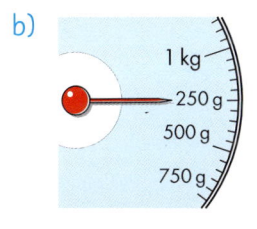

b) ☐ kg ☐ g

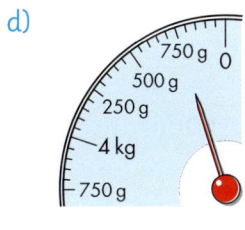

c) ☐ kg ☐ g

d) ☐ kg ☐ g

5 Now try Worksheets 4 and 5 *Reading scales (1)* and *(2)*.

UNIT 8 MEASURES

6 Here is a different scale face.

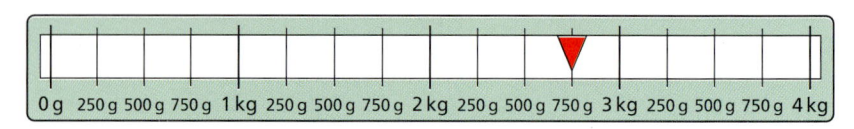

It shows 2 kg 750 g.

Write down the weights on the scales below.

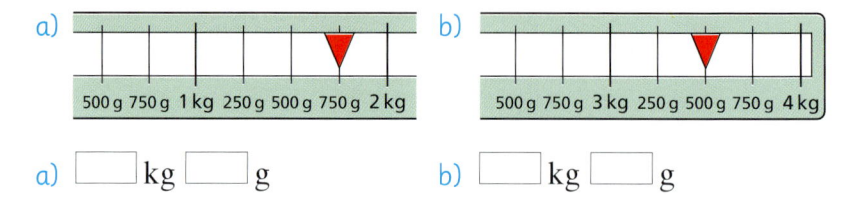

a) ☐ kg ☐ g   b) ☐ kg ☐ g

7 Try Worksheet 6 *Different scales*.

8 Write down the weights in order, **lightest** weight first.

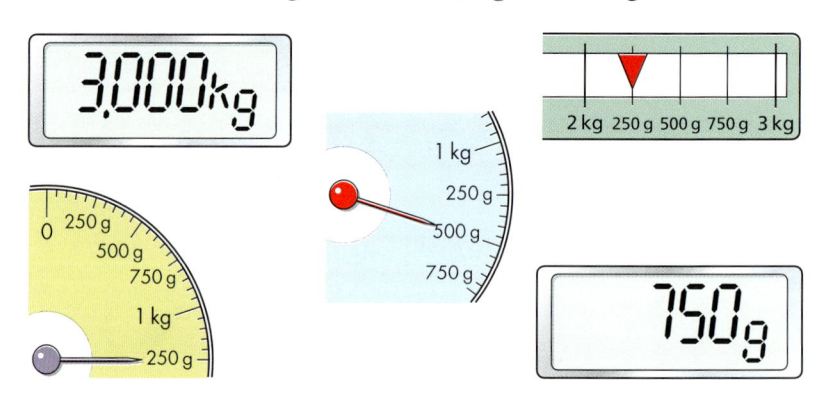

9 Choose the correct unit of measure – **grams (g)** or **kilograms (kg)**.

a)

a) We weigh in _____ .

Length and weight 91

b)

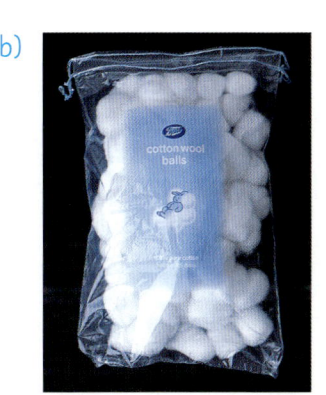

b) We weigh in _____ .

c)

c) We weigh in _____ .

d)

d) We weigh in _____ .

Now try Unit 8 Test.

Review 8

1. Add these numbers.
   Then write them to the **nearest hundred** and add them.

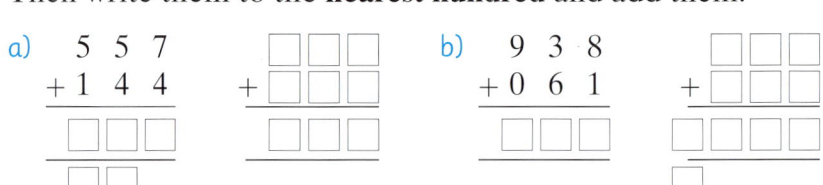

   a) 5 5 7
     + 1 4 4
     ‾‾‾‾‾

     + ☐☐☐
       ☐☐☐
       ‾‾‾
       ☐☐☐

   b) 9 3 8
     + 0 6 1
     ‾‾‾‾‾

     + ☐☐☐
       ☐☐☐
       ‾‾‾
       ☐☐☐☐

2. Write in **digits**:

   a) one hundred and eighty-two

   b) ten thousand one hundred and two

   c) one thousand and eighty

3. a) Write in order – smallest decimal number first.

   0.30   0.07   0.70   0.03

   b) Write as decimals:

   $\frac{5}{10} = \square.\square\square$ $\frac{5}{100} = \square.\square\square$

4. Sal has **£45**.

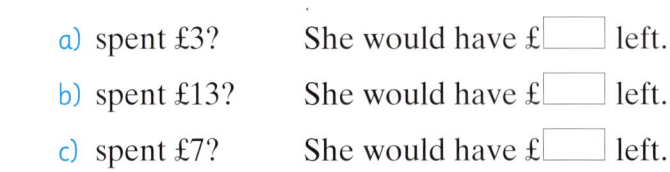

   How much would she have left if she:

   a) spent £3?   She would have £☐ left.

   b) spent £13?   She would have £☐ left.

   c) spent £7?   She would have £☐ left.

   d) spent £38?   She would have £☐ left.

5. Write the times in words.

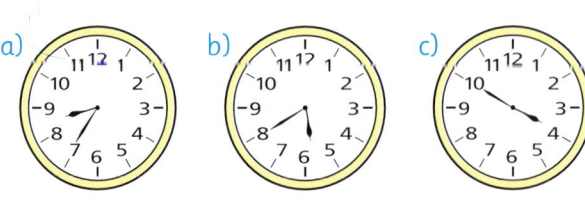

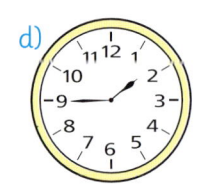

   a)   b)   c)   d)

9 Number

Subtraction to 1000

Unit 9 words

figures	count on	count back
number line	pound (£)	pence (p)
nearer to	hundred	minus
nearest ten	nearest hundred	plus

Remember

Examples are shown in red.

means copy and complete.

You need
- a set of Unit 9 vocabulary Snap cards.

Play a game of Snap to help you learn the words.

Try the **word test** to get some points.

1 Don set out 48 − 3 in columns to help him to work out the answer.

He set it out as:
```
   4 8
 − 3
 ─────
   1 8
```

He got the **wrong** answer.

Tell your partner or teacher where Don went wrong.

2 a) £8 − £6 = ☐ b) £18 − £6 = ☐
   c) £28 − £6 = ☐ d) £58 − £6 = ☐
   e) £9 − £5 = ☐   f) £15 − £9 = ☐
   g) £75 − £9 = ☐ h) £95 − £9 = ☐

3 Try Worksheet 1 *Jigsaw subtraction*.

Explain to a partner how you worked out the answers.
You can use base 10 blocks if you wish to help you.

4 a) 52 − 36 = ☐   b) 156 − 72 = ☐

5 Lin works in a shop. She sells biscuits.
She has:

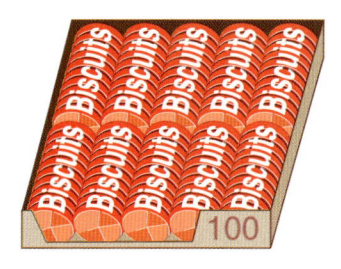

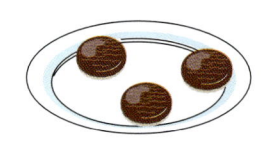

Someone wants to buy **7 packets**.
Lin must open the box of 100 and put the 10 packets of ten on the shelf.
Now she has:

She sells the 7 packets.
Now she has:

Subtraction to 1000

We can show this **in figures**.

```
                    12 packets on the shelf
                            ↓
0 boxes left    →    0  ₁
                     ↙ 2 3  ←  3 singles on plate
7 packets sold  →  –   7 0  ←  0 singles eaten
5 packets left  →    5 3   ←  3 singles left
```

Another day, she has **one box** and **two packets** of biscuits on the shelf.
Will she need to open the box to get more packets if she wants to sell:

a) 5 packets?   b) 7 packets?   c) 1 packet?   d) 2 packets?
Answer **Yes** or **No**.

How many boxes would she have left each time?

e) ☐ boxes   f) ☐ boxes   g) ☐ boxes   h) ☐ boxes

6 You may need

- base ten blocks to help you.

Set out your work to show where you opened a **box** or a **packet**.

> **Remember**
>
> The **top line** shows the biscuits on the counter
> **before** the singles were eaten or the packets sold.

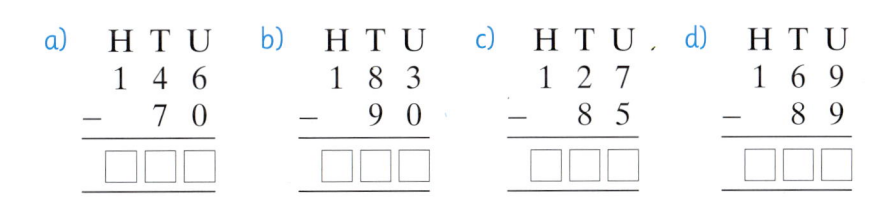

a) H T U   b) H T U   c) H T U   d) H T U
    1 4 6   1 8 3   1 2 7   1 6 9
  –   7 0   –   9 0   –   8 5   –   8 9
    ☐ ☐ ☐   ☐ ☐ ☐   ☐ ☐ ☐   ☐ ☐ ☐

7 Use the **number line** to help you complete the following.

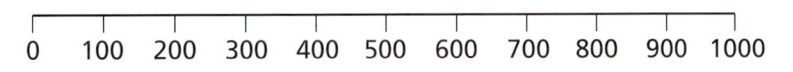

```
|----|----|----|----|----|----|----|----|----|----|
0   100  200  300  400  500  600  700  800  900  1000
```

a) 900 – 300 = ☐   b) 1000 – 300 = ☐

UNIT 9 NUMBER

8 a) H T U
       2 4 6
   −   7 0

b) H T U
   3 8 3
− 1 9 0

c) H T U
   4 2 7
− 2 8 5

d) H T U
   3 6 9
− 2 8 9

9 You may need
- base 10 blocks to help you.

If Lin had:

and someone wanted to eat **one single biscuit**,
write down or tell your teacher what she would have to do.

10 We can show this **in figures**.

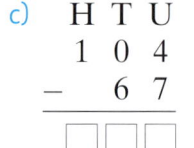

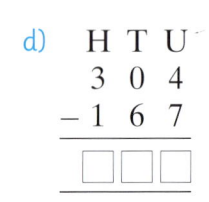

1 box opened → 1 ¹0 ¹0 ← 10 singles on plate
10 packets of ten   −   0 1 ← 1 single eaten
0 boxes left → 0 9 9 ← 9 singles left
                  ↑
        9 packets left

(above the 1: 1 packet opened, 9 packets left)

a) H T U
   1 0 0
−   7

b) H T U
   1 0 4
−   7

c) H T U
   1 0 4
−   6 7

d) H T U
   3 0 4
− 1 6 7

Subtraction to 1000   97

11 Try Worksheet 2 *Opening up*.

12 John goes shopping.
He has £123.

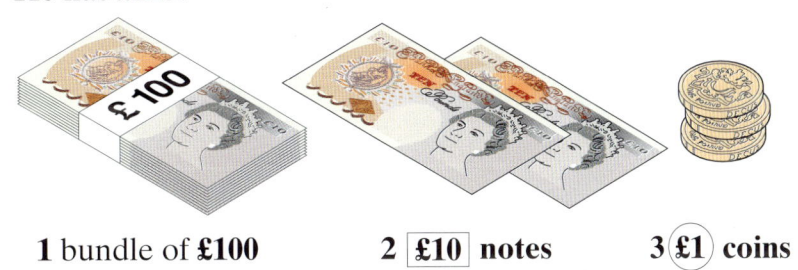

1 bundle of **£100**   **2** **£10** notes   **3** **£1** coins

John spends **£70** or **seven** **£10** notes.
To pay, he opens the bundle and takes out the **ten** **£10** notes.
Now he has

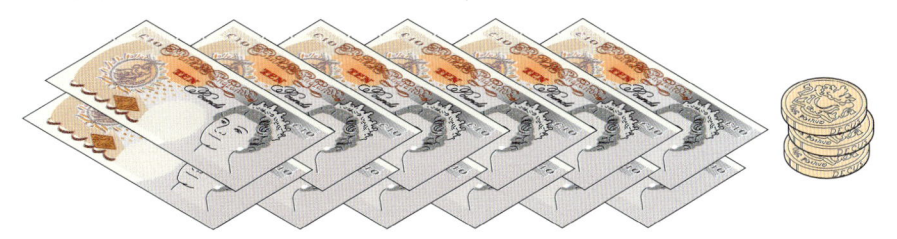

He gives the shopkeeper **seven** **£10** notes.
He has this money left.

£53

We can show this **in figures** like this.

```
       0 1
  £ 1 2 3
 −£   7 0
  £   5 3
```

Would John need to open the **bundle of £100** if he spent:

a) £50?   b) £10?   c) £30?   d) £20?

Answer **Yes** or **No**.

UNIT 9 NUMBER

13 Try Worksheet 3 *Spending money*.

14 You need
- a calculator.

Remember
There are **100p** in **£1**.

When you spend money you can work out your change in **different ways**.
You can **count on** using money.
Suppose you spend 43p and pay with a pound.
You would get this change.

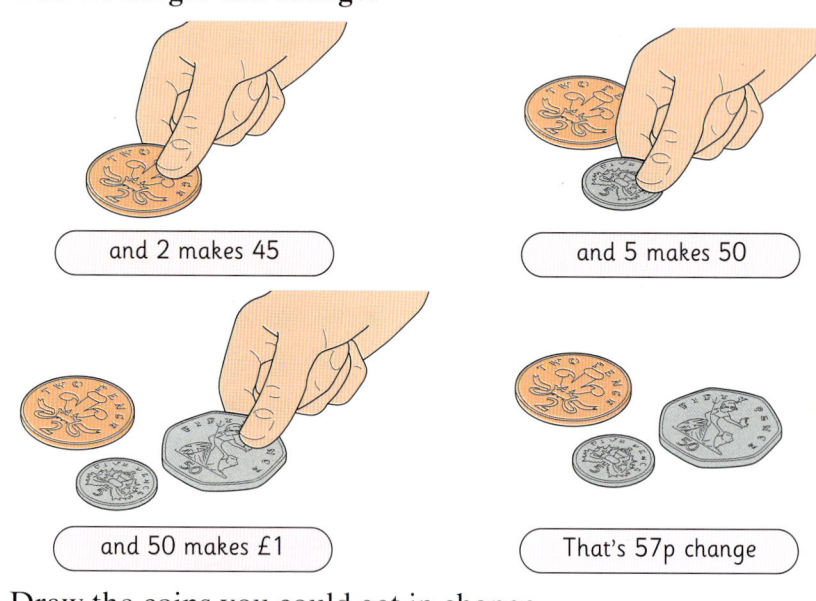

and 2 makes 45

and 5 makes 50

and 50 makes £1

That's 57p change

Draw the coins you could get in change,

(1p) (2p) (5p) (10p) (20p) (50p)

if you pay with (£1) and spend:

a) 62p   b) 71p   c) 45p   d) 38p   e) 14p   f) 97p

15 Or you can use a calculator.

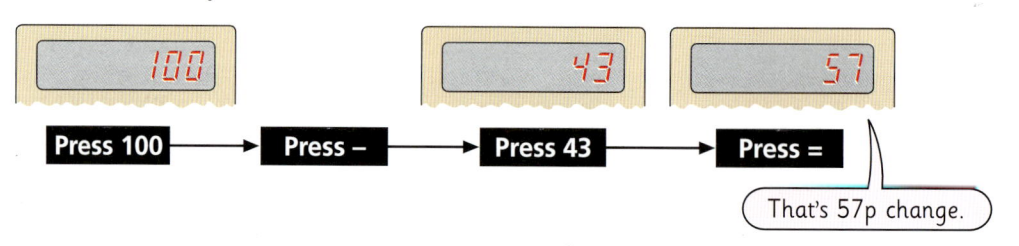

Press 100 → Press − → Press 43 → Press =

That's 57p change.

Check all your answers to **Question 14** using your calculator.

Subtraction to 1000   99

16 Work out these subtraction sums.
You can **count on** to help you like David.

David tries to do the sum 50 − 17.

He gets this far.
$$\begin{array}{r} \overset{4}{\cancel{5}}\overset{1}{0} \\ -\ 1\ 7 \\ \hline \end{array}$$

Then he gets stuck.

*I'm stuck. I can't remember the answer to **10 − 7**.*

*Try counting on like this: 7 and **how many more** make 10? 7 and **1** is 8 and **1** is 9 and **1** is 10. 7 and **3** makes 10. The answer is **3**.*

Now David does the sum like this.

(1 and how many more make 4?) $\begin{array}{r} \overset{4}{\cancel{5}}\overset{1}{0} \\ -\ 1\ 7 \\ \hline 3\ 3 \end{array}$ (7 and how many more make 10?)

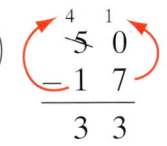

a) 60 − 17   b) 550 − 17   c) 52 − 17   d) 452 − 127

17 Draw how many of these you could get in change,

£1   £10

if you pay with £100 and spend:

a) £62   b) £71   c) £45   d) £38   e) £14   f) £97

g) Check your answers on a calculator.

How are the answers to **this** check and the check for **Question 14** different?

UNIT 9 NUMBER

Remember

Keep your eye on the **tens** digit.

Then look at the **units** digit beside it.

Remember

Keep your eye on the **hundreds** digit.

Then look at the **tens** digit beside it.

18 Write these amounts of money **roughly** to the **nearest ten**.

£1(2)6   is nearer £130 than £120.

a) £226   b) £326   c) £526   d) £926

Now write them **roughly** to the **nearest hundred**.

£(1)26   is nearer £100 than £200.

19 Subtract these amounts of money.
Then write them to the **nearest ten** and subtract again.

```
   ¹  ¹                ¹  ¹
£  2  2  6        £  2  3  0
-£    4  3        -£ 1  4  0
─────────         ─────────
£  0  8  3        £  0  9  0
```

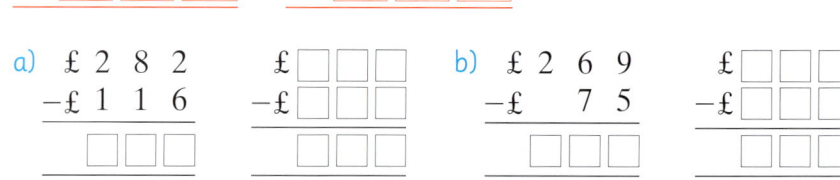

a)   £ 2 8 2   £ ☐☐☐   b)   £ 2 6 9   £ ☐☐☐
    -£ 1 1 6   -£ ☐☐☐   -£   7 5   -£ ☐☐☐
    ───────   ───────   ───────   ───────
      ☐☐☐   ☐☐☐   ☐☐☐   ☐☐☐

20 Now try Worksheet 4 *Subtract roughly (1)*.

21 Subtract these amounts.
Then write them to the **nearest hundred** and subtract again.

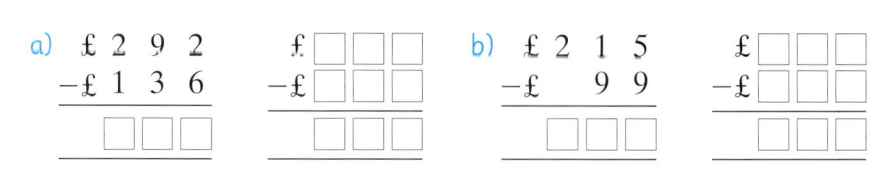

```
   ¹  ¹
£  2  2  6        £  2  0  0
-£ 1  4  3        -£ 1  0  0
─────────         ─────────
£  0  8  3        £  1  0  0
```

a)   £ 2 9 2   £ ☐☐☐   b)   £ 2 1 5   £ ☐☐☐
    -£ 1 3 6   -£ ☐☐☐   -£   9 9   -£ ☐☐☐
    ───────   ───────   ───────   ───────
      ☐☐☐   ☐☐☐   ☐☐☐   ☐☐☐

Subtraction to 1000 101

22 Now try Worksheet 5 *Subtract roughly (2)*.

23 This is a photo of a family party. There are people of different ages.

(Photo labels: Carl 28, Bet 48, Ella 9 months, Annie 90, Fin 19, Ben 51, Kate 3, Mia 30, Joe 1, Patrick 2, Jeannie 23)

a) Joe is ☐ years **younger** than Kate.

b) Kate is ☐ years **older** than Joe.

c) The **difference** in their ages is ☐ years.

Patrick is:

d) ☐ years **younger** than Fin.

e) ☐ years **younger** than Carl.

f) ☐ years **older** than Joe.

g) ☐ years **younger** than Annie.

The **difference** in Jeannie's age and

h) Bet's is ☐ years. i) Fin's is ☐ years.

j) Ben's is ☐ years. k) Annie's is ☐ years.

l) Mia's is ☐ years.

24 Find out what a **generation** means.
How many generations are there in the photograph in **Question 23**.
What age would Kate, Fin, Bet, Mia and Jeannie be if they were:

a) 10 years **older**? b) 9 years **older**?

c) 10 years **younger**? d) 9 years **younger**?

e) Ella is ☐ months younger than Joe.

25 Rose cuts these pieces of wood in DT.

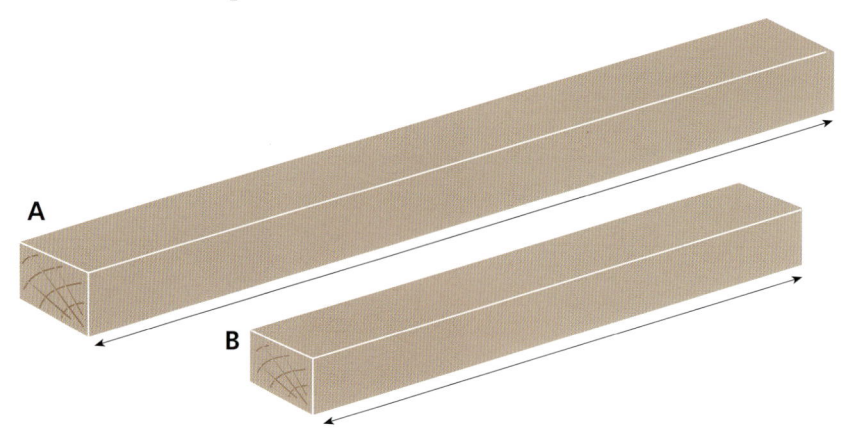

a) Block A is ☐ mm **longer** than Block B.

b) Block B is ☐ mm **shorter** than Block A.

c) The **difference** in the length of the blocks is ☐ mm.

d) Draw a line 15 mm **shorter** than the length of Block A.

e) Draw a line 78 mm **longer** than the length of Block B.

f) How many millimetres difference is there in the lines you have drawn?

26 You may need
- a calculator.

Find the missing answers to complete the patterns.

Does it matter about the order in which you put the numbers into the calculator?

a) 300 + 1 = ☐
   300 − 1 = ☐
   300 + 10 = ☐
   300 − 10 = ☐
   300 + 100 = ☐
   300 − 100 = ☐

b) 310 + 1 = ☐
   310 − 1 = ☐
   310 + 10 = ☐
   310 − 10 = ☐
   310 + 100 = ☐
   310 − 100 = ☐

Now try Unit 9 Test.

Review 9

1. Pick out the **even** numbers and add them together.
   a) 3   6   7   8   9
   b) 352   435   127   318   249

2. Fill in the missing numbers.

×	2	3	4	5	10
7		21			
2			8	10	
9	18		36		

×	3	10	5	2	4
7		70			
2			10	4	
9	27		45		

3. Divide and write remainders where there are any.
   a) 28 ÷ 5 = ☐
   b) 98 ÷ 10 = ☐
   c) 19 ÷ 2 = ☐
   d) 39 ÷ 5 = ☐
   e) 20 ÷ 2 = ☐
   f) 40 ÷ 10 = ☐

4. Look at the calendar showing the month of June. Which **days** in June are the following dates?

JUNE						
Mon	Tue	Wed	Thurs	Fri	Sat	Sun
	1	2	3	4	5	6
7	8	9	10	11	12	13
14	15	16	17	18	19	20
21	22	23	24	25	26	27
28	29	30				

   a) 4th   b) 18th   c) 22nd   d) 27th   e) 30th
   f) What dates are the Saturdays?
   g) The date four days before the 17th June is the ☐th June.
   h) The 1st July will be a _____ .
   i) The 31st May was a _____ .

10 Measures
Area

Unit 10 words

area	covers	space
square centimetre (sq cm)	square metre (sq m)	same size
exact	roughly	right angle
about	divide	equal

Remember

Examples are shown in red.

✏️ means copy and complete.

You need
- a set of Unit 9 vocabulary Snap cards.

Play a game of Snap to help you learn the words.

Try the **word test** to get some points.

1   The amount of **space** something **covers** is called the **area**. For example, the area of a table top could be seen as the amount of cloth it would take to cover the surface exactly.

Area 105

You need
- newspaper
- scissors.

a) Cut out paper to show the area of three surfaces in your classroom.

b) Talk or write about areas you might need to find around your house in order to do certain jobs.

2   We measure **areas** in **squares**.
Jason and Jade are going to tile the area of the wall above the sinks in their kitchens.

Jason's sink   Jade's sink

They each use different square tiles.

UNIT 10 MEASURES

Count the square tiles on each wall.

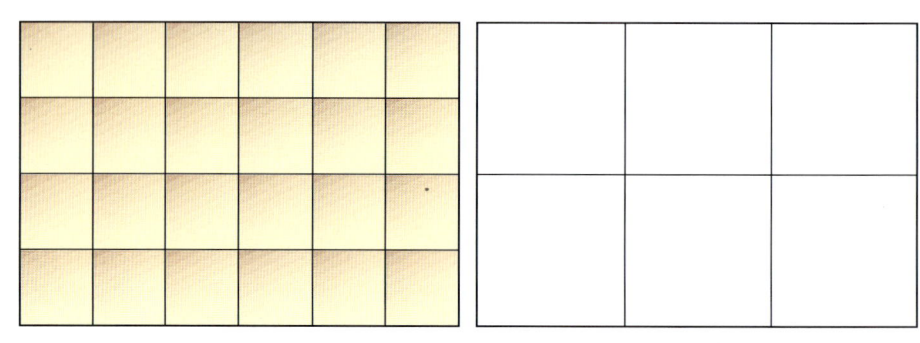

Jason's wall   Jade's wall

a) Jason's wall takes ☐ squares.

b) Jade's wall takes ☐ squares.

c) Is Jason's wall **larger**, **smaller** or the **same** area as Jade's wall?

Comment on your answer.

3 To find areas, we need to use **squares** which are the **same size**.

We use a square like this:

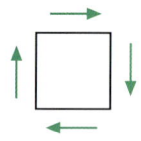

Measure the sides of the square above.

Each side is ☐ centimetre long.

Remember

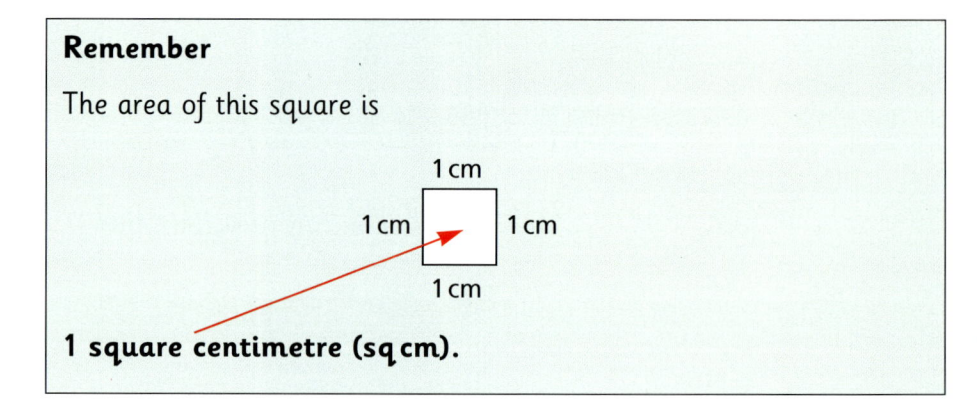

The area of this square is

1 cm
1 cm   1 cm
1 cm

1 square centimetre (sq cm).

Area 107

4 This shape covers an **area** of **6 square centimetres (sq cm).**

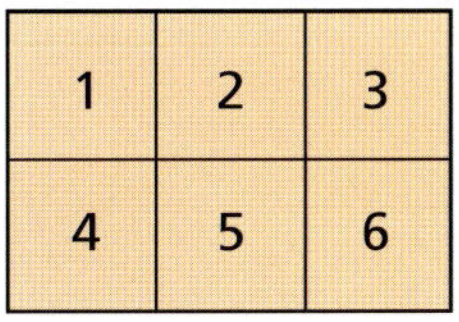

1	2	3
4	5	6

What areas do these shapes cover?

a)

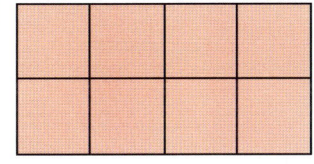

b)

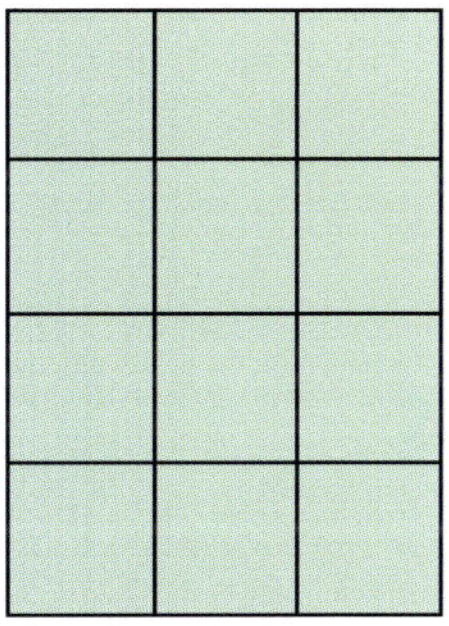

a) ☐ sq cm   b) ☐ sq cm

c)

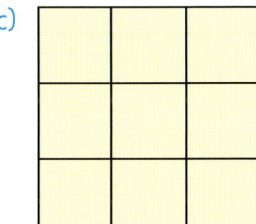

c) ☐ sq cm

5 Try Worksheet 1 *Count the squares*.

6 To find an area like this with no squares showing,

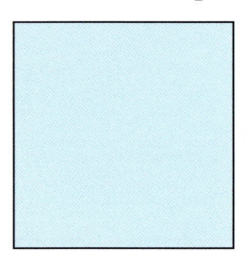

you can use a clear plastic grid like this:

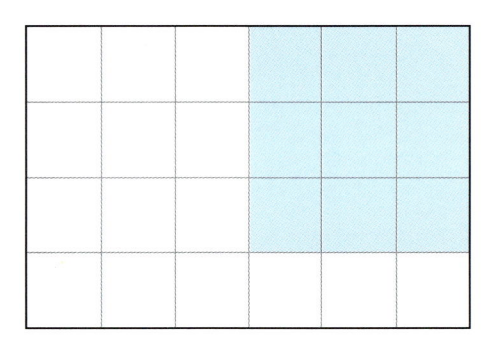

The area of the blue square is 9 square centimetres (sq cm).

You need

- a clear plastic grid.

Find the areas of these shapes.

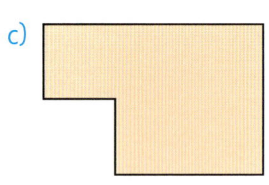

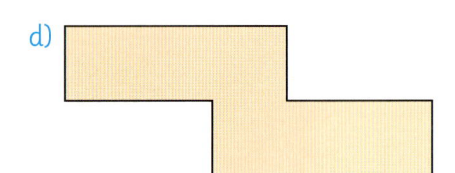

a)

b)

a) Area = ☐ sq cm   b) Area = ☐ sq cm

c)

d)

c) Area = ☐ sq cm   d) Area = ☐ sq cm

7 Try Worksheet 3 *Find the area*.

Area 109

8 You need
- a clear plastic grid.

Sometimes it is not easy to find the area of something like this.

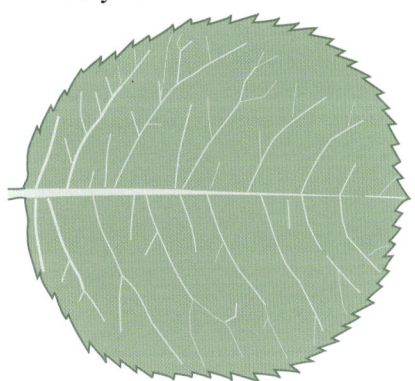

We can use a plastic grid to help find the area **roughly**.

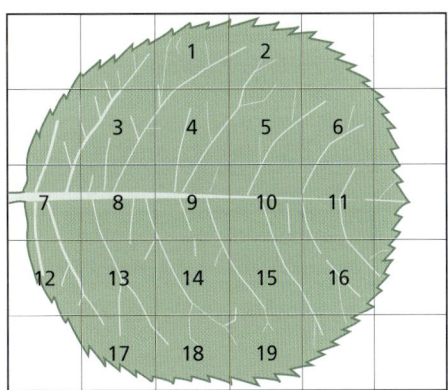

Remember

Count only **whole** squares and squares which are **more than a half**.

The area of this leaf is **roughly 19 square centimetres**.
Use a clear grid to find the area of these leaves.

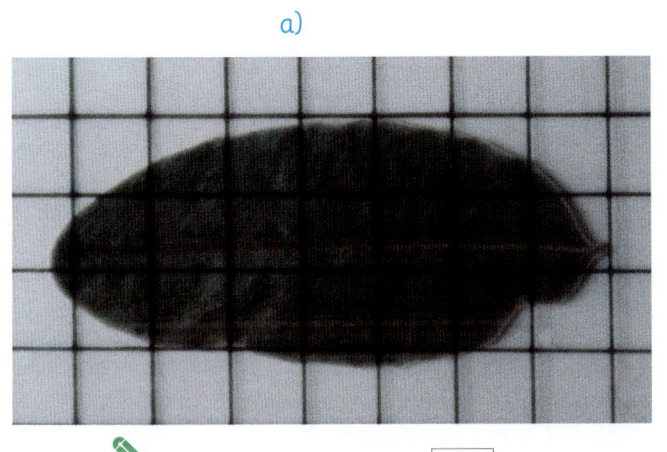

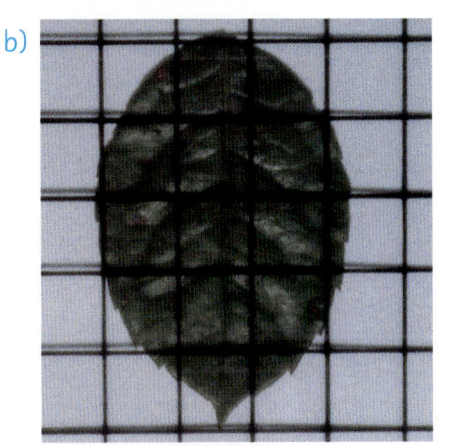

a)

b)

a) Area = ☐ sq cm   b) Area = ☐ sq cm

UNIT 10 MEASURES

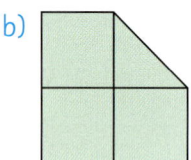

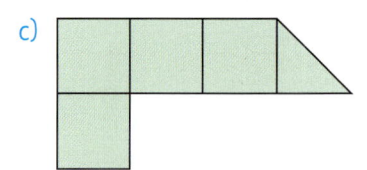

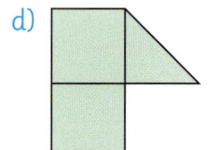

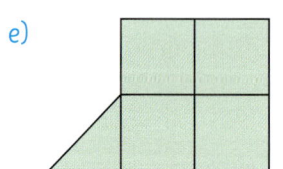

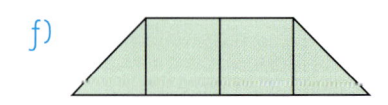

9   Try Worksheet 4 *Leafy areas*.

10 This square centimetre has been divided into **two equal triangles**.

> **Remember**
>
> The area of the **whole square** is **1 square centimetre** (1 sq cm).

The area of this triangle is _____ a square centimetre.

The area of this shape is $3\frac{1}{2}$ square centimetres.

1	2
3	$\frac{1}{2}$

> **Remember**
>
> **Two half** squares make **one whole**.
>
> We count each of these triangles as a **half ($\frac{1}{2}$) square centimetre**.

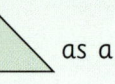

Work out the areas of these shapes.

a) Area = $1\frac{1}{2}$ sq cm

b)

c)

d)

e)

f)

Area 111

11 Try Worksheet 5 *Areas in halves*.

12 You need

- 4 metre rules
- newspaper/sugar paper
- scissors/cellotape
- chalk.

We measure **larger** areas in **square metres (sq m)**.
Cut out some of your own paper **square metres (sq m)**.

Use metre rules to help.
Make sure the corners are **right angles**.
Find the **rough area** of:

a) a floor or part of a floor   b) a wall or part of a wall.

13 Which squares would you use to measure the following –
square centimetres (sq cm) or **square metres** (sq m)?
I would measure the area of:

a) a carpet in _____ _____ .

b) a cushion cover in _____ _____ .

c) glass for a photo frame in _____ _____ .

d) a playground in _____ _____ .

14 Try Worksheet Puzzle *Border areas*.

Now try Unit 10 Test.

Review 10

1. Write in **words**.

   a) 1029   b) 10 009   c) 92

2. a) 2 5 9   b) 2 4 5   c) 1 1 9   d) 7 1 9
      +   5 4   + 2 8 2   + 7 4 7   + 2 8 1

3. a) 0 . 4   b) 0 . 8   c) 1 . 6   d) 1 . 5   e) 2 . 6
      + 0 . 5   + 0 . 8   + 0 . 8   + 1 . 2   + 1 . 4
       □ . □   □ . □   □ . □   □ . □   □ . □
                      □   □   □

4. Measure each of these hems in **decimal centimetres** and **millimetres**.

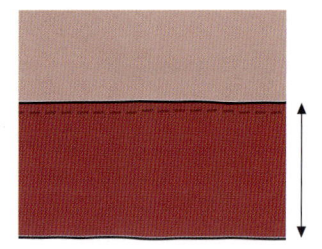

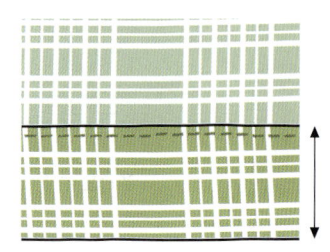

   a) □.□ cm **or** □ mm   b) □.□ cm **or** □ mm

5. Subtract these amounts of money.
   Then write them to the **nearest ten** and subtract again.

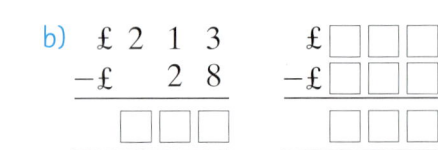

   a) £ 5 6 2   £ □□□   b) £ 2 1 3   £ □□□
       −£ 1 5 8   −£ □□□   −£   2 8   −£ □□□
         □□□   □□□   □□□   □□□

   Subtract these amounts.
   Then write them to the **nearest hundred** and subtract again.

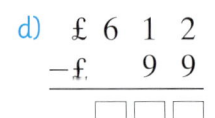

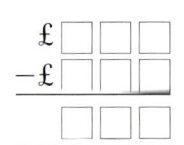

   c) £ 3 9 0   £ □□□   d) £ 6 1 2   £ □□□
       £ 1 5 0   −£ □□□   −£   9 9   −£ □□□
         □□□   □□□   □□□   □□□

11 Number

Division by 2, 3, 4, 5 and 10

Unit 11 words

shared	equally	halve
share	each	between
quarter	left over	figures
different	remainder	whole

Remember

Examples are shown in red.

✎ means copy and complete.

You need
- a set of Unit 9 vocabulary Snap cards.

Play a game of Snap to help you learn the words.

Try the **word test** to get some points.

1 A group of friends have a barbecue.

114 UNIT 11 NUMBER

They share **16** sausages equally.

They each get

16 sausages shared between 4 people gives 4 sausages each.

a) Twenty-four sausages shared between 4 people gives ☐ sausages each.

24 ÷ 4 = ☐

b) Eight sausages shared between 4 people gives ☐ sausages each.

8 ÷ 4 = ☐

c) Twenty sausages shared between 4 people gives ☐ sausages each.

20 ÷ 4 = ☐

d) Thirty-six sausages shared between 4 people gives ☐ sausages each.

36 ÷ 4 = ☐

2 a) 4 8 12 16 ☐ ☐ ☐ ☐ ☐ ☐

b) 4 ☐ 12 ☐ 20 ☐ 28 ☐ 36 ☐

c) 4 8 ☐ 16 ☐ ☐ 28 ☐ ☐ 40

3 Try Worksheet 1 *Four shares*.

You need
- a 30 cm ruler.

Division by 2, 3, 4, 5 and 10 • 115

4   How many jumps of **4** are there to reach 20?
    You can use your ruler to help you.

    0 1 2 3 4 5 6 7 8 9 10 11 12 13 14 15 16 17 18 19 20

   a) It takes ☐ jumps of 4 to reach 20.
   b) It takes ☐ jumps of 4 to reach 12.
   c) It takes ☐ jumps of 4 to reach 28.
   d) It takes ☐ jumps of 4 to reach 8.
   e) It takes ☐ jumps of 4 to reach 16.
   f) It takes ☐ jumps of 4 to reach 32.
   g) It takes ☐ jumps of 4 to reach 40.

5   Find a $\frac{1}{4}$ (quarter) of these pens.

   a) $\frac{1}{4}$ of 16 pens = ☐   b) $\frac{1}{4}$ of 8 pens = ☐
   c) $\frac{1}{4}$ of 24 pens = ☐   d) $\frac{1}{4}$ of 12 pens = ☐
   e) $\frac{1}{4}$ of 28 pens = ☐   f) $\frac{1}{4}$ of 20 pens = ☐

Remember

To find a $\frac{1}{4}$ (quarter) of something, you **divide by 4**.

6

I don't know what 24 divided by 4 is!

*But, you **do** know how many **fours** make 24.*

*Of course, **6** fours make **24**. So the answer to 24 ÷ 4 is **6**.*

a) ☐ × 4 = 24   b) 24 ÷ 4 = ☐   c) ☐ × 4 = 16   d) 16 ÷ 4 = ☐
e) ☐ × 4 = 36   f) 36 ÷ 4 = ☐   g) ☐ × 4 = 12   h) 12 ÷ 4 = ☐
i) ☐ × 4 = 20   j) 20 ÷ 4 = ☐   k) ☐ × 4 = 40   l) 40 ÷ 4 = ☐
m) ☐ × 4 = 28   n) 28 ÷ 4 = ☐

7 Tim bought 10 burgers.
He shares them with 3 friends.

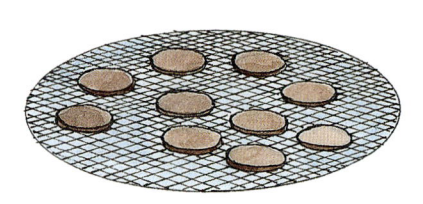

They each get

10 burgers shared between 4 people gives 2 whole burgers each.

a) There are ☐ burgers left over.

b) How could they share the left over burgers?

8 Copy and complete the table below.

a) Write how many sausages each get and how many are left over.

	Number each	Sausages left over
20 sausages ÷ 4	5 sausages	0
21 sausages ÷ 4		
22 sausages ÷ 4		
10 sausages ÷ 4		
11 sausages ÷ 4		
12 sausages ÷ 4		
15 sausages ÷ 4		
16 sausages ÷ 4		
17 sausages ÷ 4		

b) What is the largest number of sausages they could have left over?

9 Try Worksheet 2 *Three shares*.

Division by 2, 3, 4, 5 and 10 • 117

10 Try Worksheet 3 *Jigsaw division*.

11 When we share 8 single biscuits between 4 people, we can show this in figures:

$$8 \div 4 = \boxed{2} \quad \text{or} \quad 4\overline{)8}^{\;\boxed{2}}$$

a) $6 \div 3 = \Box$ b) $8 \div 2 = \Box$ c) $5 \div 5 = \Box$

d) $3\overline{)6}^{\;\Box}$ e) $2\overline{)8}^{\;\Box}$ f) $5\overline{)5}^{\;\Box}$

12 When we share **1 packet** of ten biscuits between **2** people we need to open the packet like this.

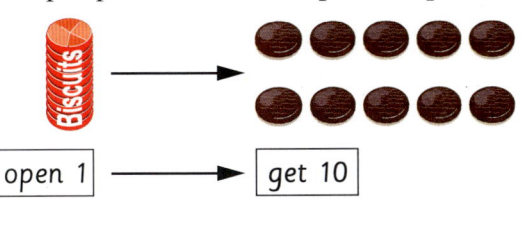

open 1 ⟶ get 10

We can write this as:

$$10 \div 2 = 5 \quad \text{or} \quad 2\overline{)1\,{}^{1}0}^{\;\;\text{T U}\;5}$$

a) $10 \div 5 = \Box$ b) $12 \div 2 = \Box$ c) $16 \div 4 = \Box$

In the sums below, show when you opened a packet.

d) T U
$\Box\Box$
$5\overline{)1\;0}$

e) T U
$\Box\Box$
$2\overline{)1\;2}$

f) T U
$\Box\Box$
$4\overline{)1\;6}$

g) What do you think is wrong with this answer?

T U
5
$2\overline{)1\;0}$

UNIT 11 NUMBER

13 Try Worksheet 4 *Left overs*.

14 When we share 2 packets of biscuits between 2 people,

Remember
There are **10** single biscuits in **1** packet of ten.

each person will get

We can write this as: 20 ÷ 2 = 10

or show when we opened a packet like this:

```
   T U
   1 0
2)2 0
```

a) 30 ÷ 3 = ☐   b) 50 ÷ 5 = ☐   c) 40 ÷ 4 = ☐

d) T U   e) T U   f) T U
    ☐☐   ☐☐   ☐☐
 3)3 0   5)5 0   4)4 0

15 When we share 1 packet of ten biscuits and 1 biscuit

between 2 people we need to open the packet like this:

```
     T U
     0 5 r1
  2)1¹1
```

We can write this as: 11 ÷ 2 = 5 r1   or

a) 11 ÷ 5 = ☐ r ☐   b) 13 ÷ 2 = ☐ r ☐   c) 18 ÷ 4 = ☐ r ☐

Show when you opened a packet.

d) T U   e) T U   f) T U
    ☐☐ r ☐   ☐☐ r ☐   ☐☐ r ☐
 5)1 1   2)1 3   4)1 8

Division by 2, 3, 4, 5 and 10 • 119

16 a) What would you need to do if you wanted to share **2 packets** of Biscuits between **4 people**?

b) How many biscuits do each get?
c) Are there any left over?

We can write this as:

$$20 \div 4 = 5 \quad \text{or} \quad 4\overline{)2\,{}^{2}0} \;\; \begin{array}{c} T\ U \\ 0\ 5 \end{array}$$

d) $20 \div 5 = \square$

e) $30 \div 5 = \square$

f) $\begin{array}{c} T\ U \\ \square\square \\ 5\overline{)2\ 0} \end{array}$

g) $\begin{array}{c} T\ U \\ \square\square \\ 5\overline{)3\ 0} \end{array}$

17 If we shared this money between 3 people,

we would do it like this.

$$£12 \div 3 = £4 \quad \text{or} \quad 3\overline{)£\,{}^{1}1\,{}^{1}2} \;\; \begin{array}{c} £\ 0\ 4 \end{array}$$

Share the following money between **three** people.
Show in figures – in **two ways** – how much each would get.

a)

b)

120 UNIT 11 NUMBER

Remember

Share the money between **3 people**.

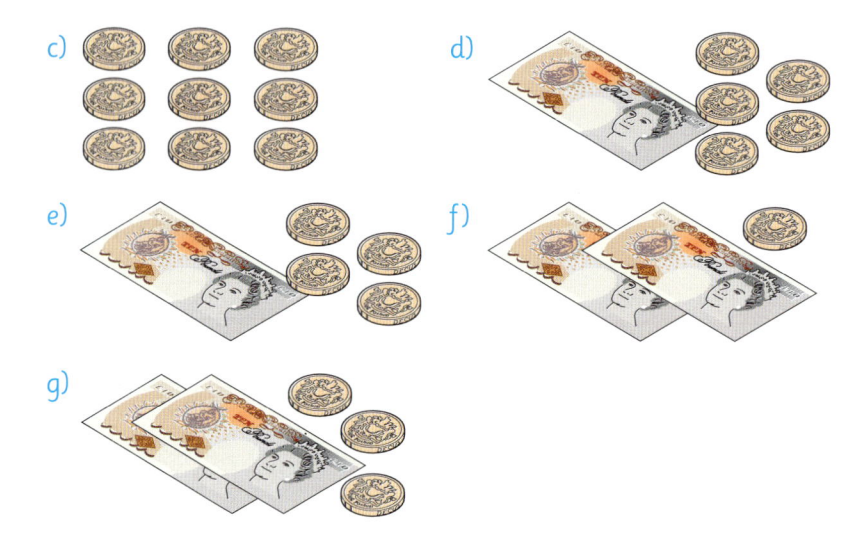

c)

d)

e)

f)

g)

18 Try Worksheet 5 *More shares*.

19 You may need

- a calculator
- notes and coins.

Tina and Jess go out for a special meal.

This is the bill which they halve.
They pay a **half** ($\frac{1}{2}$) each.

Starters	£4.20
Main courses	£18.00
Desserts	£4.00
Coffees	£2.16
Drinks	£6.18
Service charge	£4.00
Total	**£38.54**

They want to know what **half of the bill for each item** is.

Division by 2, 3, 4, 5 and 10

They could work it out in **three** different ways.
Jess used a calculator.

I must remember to put in the decimal point and then use the divide (÷) button.

£4.20 ÷ 2 = £2.10

Tina uses coins. She halves them like this.

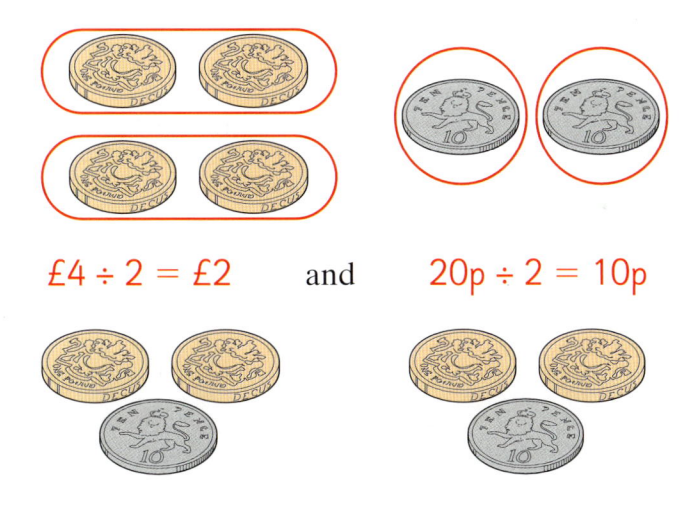

£4 ÷ 2 = £2   and   20p ÷ 2 = 10p

Each pays £2.10.

The sum on paper looks like this.

£4.20 ÷ 2 = £2.10   or $\begin{array}{r}\text{£ 2.1 0}\\ 2\overline{)\text{£ 4.2 0}}\end{array}$

a) How much did **each** of them pay for **each** item on the bill?

b) What is half of the **total bill**?

c) Can you think of a way to check that the bill is correct?

UNIT 11 NUMBER

20 You may need
- a calculator
- notes and coins.

Ben and Simon share a flat.
They are flatmates like these.

They share all the bills each week. They each pay a half ($\frac{1}{2}$).

a) What would they each pay for the following bills?
If you need to, use a calculator to work out the answers.

Remember

When you see

`6.6`

in the calculator it means £6.6<u>0</u>.

```
                Weekly bills

Rent                                      £60
Electricity                               £12
Gas                                        £6
Telephone                                 £18
Food                                      £90
Tissues/cleaning materials, etc.           £6
```

What would **each** share of these bills be if:

b) 3 people shared?   c) 4 people shared?

d) 5 people shared?   e) 10 people shared?

You cannot always share the bills easily.
Sometimes there will be **£1 coins left over**.

f) Which **total bills** are likely to stay the same?
Which would probably change?

Division by 2, 3, 4, 5 and 10 123

21 You need
- Unit 11 Race against time cards Set 1 and Set 2
- your 'My maths record' sheet.

Race against time

1. Sort the race cards – this side up. (Do not mix up Set 1 and Set 2). Take the cards one at a time. Answer as quickly as you can.

   ☐ × 3 = 21

2. Did you get it right? Look at the other side of the card.

   7

3. When you get all the answers correct, ask a friend to test you.

4. Now **Race against time**. Go for points! Ask your teacher to test and time you.

5. Now try Set 2 – this side up.

   21 ÷ 3 = ☐

Remember
3 errors = 1 point   2 errors = 2 points
1 error = 3 points   0 errors = 5 points
Answer in 1 minute with 0 errors = 7 points

Now try Unit 11 Test.

Review 11

1. Write the **coloured squares** as decimals of the whole square.

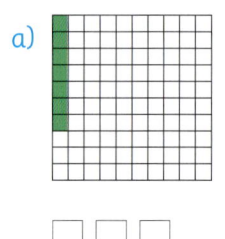

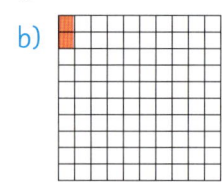

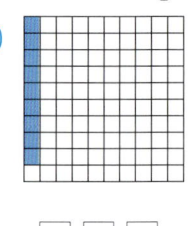

   a)   b)   c)

   ☐.☐☐   ☐.☐☐   ☐.☐☐

2. Write down the weights shown on the scales below.

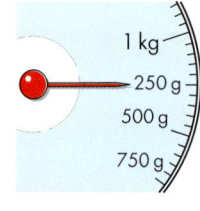

   a) ☐ kg ☐ g   b) ☐ kg ☐ g

3. Write as 24-hour clock times.

   a) 3.30 p.m.   b) 7.20 a.m.   c) 11.25 p.m.   d) 10.05 a.m.

4. Write as 12-hour clock times.

   a) 13:20   b) 07:35   c) 21:45   d) 08:05

5. **Acute**, **obtuse** or **right angle**?

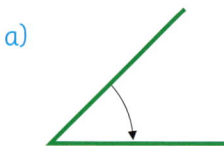

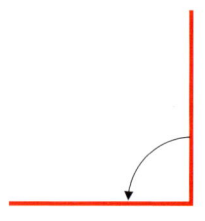

   a)   b)

   c)

12 Measures

Time: duration of time and timetables

Unit 12 words

evening	morning	past
early	late	minute
timetable	hour	between
count on	count back	quarter

Remember

Examples are shown in red.

means copy and complete.

You need
- a set of Unit 12 vocabulary Snap cards.

Play a game of Snap to help you learn the words.

Try the **word test** to get some points.

UNIT 12 MEASURES

1 You may use
- a clock face.

There are small marks on the clock between the numbers.
Each mark shows 1 minute of time.

The large hand moves through

a) ☐ minutes between the **12** and the **1**.
b) ☐ minutes between the **1** and the **2**.
c) ☐ minutes between the **2** and the **3**.
d) ☐ minutes between the **12** and the **2**.
e) ☐ minutes between the **12** and the **3**.

When the large hand moves between **1** and **5**,

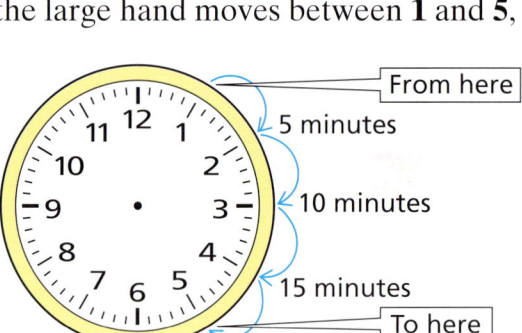

From here
5 minutes
10 minutes
15 minutes
To here
20 minutes

20 minutes have passed.

Remember

You can **count on** to find out how many minutes have passed.

2 How many minutes pass between:

a) 9.00 a.m. and 9.05 a.m.?   b) 9.05 a.m. and 9.10 a.m.?
c) 9.10 a.m. and 9.15 a.m.?   d) 9.00 a.m. and 9.10 a.m.?
e) 9.00 a.m. and 9.15 a.m.?

3 How many minutes pass between:

a) 9.10 a.m. and 9.15 a.m.?   b) 9.10 a.m. and 9.20 a.m.?
c) 9.10 a.m. and 9.25 a.m.?   d) 9.10 a.m. and 9.30 a.m.?
e) 10.10 a.m. and 10.15 a.m.?   f) 10.20 a.m. and 10.30 a.m.?
g) 10.30 a.m. and 10.40 a.m.?   h) 10.40 a.m. and 10.55 a.m.?

Time: duration of time and timetables • 127

4 Try Worksheet 1 *Minutes count*.

5 Gina works in an office.
She can take a 20-minute break between 3 o'clock and 4 o'clock.
Write down as many times as you can when she can take her break. Write the times her break **starts** and **finishes**.

   3.00 p.m.   to   3.20 p.m.

6 Fin and Jade meet at the town hall every evening for a week.

> This is the time Jade **should** arrive each day.
> But she is always **early** or **late**.

Fin says how **early** or **late** Jade was each day.
Write down the time Jade arrived
in **words**   and   as a **12-hour** clock time.

Remember

You can **count on** or **back** to find the minutes **gone** or minutes still **to go**.

a) **Monday**

> Jade is **five minutes** late.

a) She arrived at twenty past seven – 7.20 p.m.

b) **Tuesday**

> Jade is **five minutes** early.

c) **Wednesday**

> Jade is **ten minutes** early.

d) **Thursday**

> Jade is **ten minutes** late.

e) **Friday**

> Jade is **half an hour** early.

f) **Saturday**

> Jade is **half an hour** late.

g) **Sunday**

> Jade is **quarter of an hour** early.

7 Try Worksheet 2 *Early or late?*

UNIT 12 MEASURES

8 Fin and Jade are in Year 10B at school.
This is their timetable for three days.

Time	Monday	Tuesday	Wednesday
9:00–9:30	Registration/Tutor time	Registration/ assembly	Registration/PSE
9:30–10:00	English – Room 18	Maths – Room 26	Science – Lab 1
10:00–10:30	English – Room 18	Maths – Room 26	Science – Lab 1
10:30–10:45	**Break**	**Break**	**Break**
10:45–11:15	Maths – Room 26	ICT – IT1	Maths – Room 26
11:15–11:45	Maths – Room 26	English – Room 18	Maths – Room 26
11:45–12:15	History – Room 11	Art – Art Room 3	French – Room 35
12:15–13:30	**Lunchtime**	**Lunchtime**	**Lunchtime**
13:30–14:00	French – Room 35	Games	Design/Technology
14:00–14:30	Geography – Room 11	Games	Design/Technology
14:30–15:00	Music – Hall	Games	ICT – IT1

a) Science begins at ☐☐.☐☐ on Wednesday.

b) Lunchtime ends at ☐☐.☐☐ .

c) Morning break begins at ☐☐.☐☐ .

d) School finishes at ☐☐.☐☐ .

Fin arrives at **room 35**.
Which **day** and **time** could it be?

e) It is a _____ at ☐☐.☐☐ .

    or

f) It is a _____ at ☐☐.☐☐ .

On Monday:

g) History lasts for ☐ minutes.

h) English lasts for ☐ hour.

i) Break lasts for ☐ minutes.

Jade has a dental appointment at 12:00 on Wednesday.

j) She will miss her _____ lesson.

Time: duration of time and timetables 129

9 Jade lives in Bilton.
She gets the bus to school in York.
The bus stops outside her school.
These are two of her local timetables.

Harrogate to York			
Harrogate	7.00 a.m.	11.30 a.m.	2.00 p.m.
Castle Inn	7.10 a.m.	11.40 a.m.	2.10 p.m.
Thorpe	7.30 a.m.	12.00 noon	2.30 p.m.
Bilton	7.50 a.m.	12.20 p.m.	2.50 p.m.
Acomb	8.00 a.m.	12.30 p.m.	3.00 p.m.
York	8.15 a.m.	12.45 p.m.	3.15 p.m.

York to Harrogate			
York	9.45 a.m.	1.00 p.m.	3.15 p.m.
Acomb	10.00 a.m.	1.15 p.m.	3.30 p.m.
Bilton	10.10 a.m.	1.25 p.m.	3.40 p.m.
Thorpe	10.30 a.m.	1.45 p.m.	4.00 p.m.
Castle Inn	10.50 a.m.	2.05 p.m.	4.20 p.m.
Harrogate	11.00 a.m.	2.15 p.m.	4.30 p.m.

The **7.00 a.m.** from **Harrogate** stops at:

a) Castle Inn at ☐.☐☐ a.m.

b) Thorpe at ☐.☐☐ a.m.

c) Bilton at ☐.☐☐ a.m.

d) York at ☐.☐☐ a.m.

e) Jade will catch the ☐.☐☐ a.m. bus to York each morning.

f) She will arrive in York at ☐.☐☐ a.m.

Early or late?

g) She will be ☐ minutes _____ for school.

h) After school she catches the bus leaving York at ☐.☐☐ p.m.

i) She arrives at Bilton at ☐.☐☐ p.m.

j) The journey to school takes ☐ minutes.

k) The journey from York to Harrogate takes ☐ minutes.

Remember
School starts at 9.00 and finishes at 15.00

Remember
To change 12-hour to 24-hour clock times, **add 12** to the p.m. hour times – **3.00 p.m.** becomes **15:00**.

130 **UNIT 12 MEASURES**

10 Put these times in order – **earliest** time first.

a) 3.10 a.m.   16:05   15:10   4.05 a.m.   2.10 p.m.

b) | 21:45 | 02:30 | 09:45 | 14:30 |

11 Try Worksheet 3 *12- and 24-hour clock*.

12 The band **DELTA** go on tour.

DELTA is Jade and her friend Kev's favourite band. They see this notice in the paper.

δ DELTA δ
BRITISH TOUR

Belfast – July 24th at 7.45 p.m.

London – July 5th at 8.15 p.m.

Glasgow – July 19th at 7.30 p.m.

Cardiff – July 15th at 7.00 p.m.

a) The **first** concert is in _____ .

b) The **second** concert is in _____ .

c) The **third** concert is in _____ .

Time: duration of time and timetables • 131

d) The **fourth** concert is in _____ .

e) The concert starts **earliest** in _____
at ☐.☐☐ p.m.

f) The concert starts **latest** in _____
at ☐.☐☐ p.m.

g) The concert in _____ starts at 19:30.

Each concert lasts for **1½ hours**.

Write the times they finish as 12-hour **and** 24-hour times.

The concert will finish in:

h) London at ☐.☐☐ p.m. or ☐.☐☐ .

i) Glasgow at ☐.☐☐ p.m. or ☐.☐☐ .

j) Cardiff at ☐.☐☐ p.m. or ☐.☐☐ .

k) Belfast at ☐.☐☐ p.m. or ☐.☐☐ .

13 Try Worksheet 4 *Concert calendar*.

14 Kevin borrows a camcorder.
He can take a video for **1 hour (60 minutes)** before the tape runs out.
You can see on the screen the number of **minutes used**.

To find out how many minutes are **left**, you could count on in **5**'s like this:

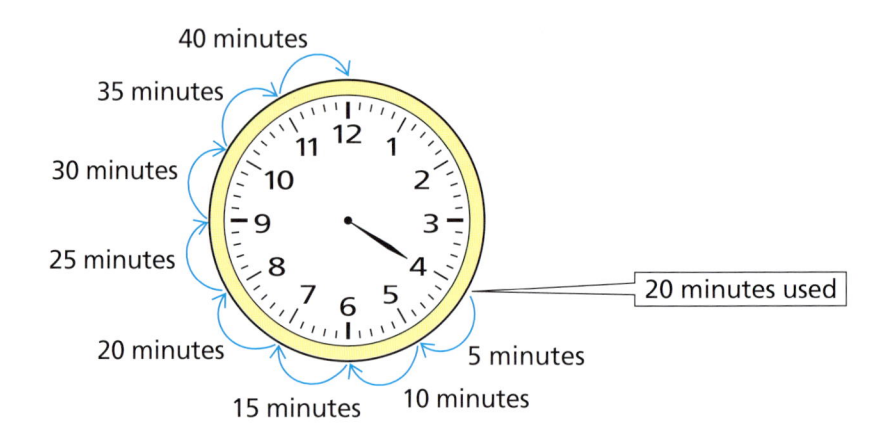

(clock face showing 20 minutes used, with counting around: 5 minutes, 10 minutes, 15 minutes, 20 minutes, 25 minutes, 30 minutes, 35 minutes, 40 minutes)

You would have **40 minutes** left.

You may need

- a watch or a clock face.

How many minutes are left:

a) if Kevin tapes for 15 minutes?

b) if he tapes for 25 minutes?

15 Try Worksheet 5 *Minutes left*.

16 The concert ($1\frac{1}{2}$ hours long) is also shown on television. Jade wants her mother to tape it for her when she is away. She has 60 minute, 120 minute and 180 minute tapes.

> **Remember**
> There are **60 minutes** in an hour.

a) Which tapes could her mother use?

b) How many hours are on each tape?

Time: duration of time and timetables 133

17 Look at the TV programmes for a Wednesday below.

BBC1	BBC2	ITV	Channel 4	Channel 5
5.35 Neighbours	5.30 Today's the Day	5.10 Home and Away	5.30 Pet Rescue	5.10 The Roseanne Show
6.00 News	6.00 Star Trek	5.40 News and Weather	6.00 Party of Five	6.00 100 Per Cent
6.30 Regional News Magazine	6.45 Sliders	5.50 Local News and Weather	6.45 Fresh Pop	6.30 Family Affairs
7.00 Style Challenge	7.30 Leviathan	6.00 Regional News Magazine	7.00 Channel 4 News	7.00 5 News
7.30 Tomorrow's World	8.00 The House Detectives	6.30 Tonight	8.00 Brookside	7.30 The Pepsi Chart
8.00 National Lottery Draw	8.30 Home Front	7.00 Emmerdale	8.30 Chef for a Night	8.00 Hot Property
8.30 Question of Sport	9.00 Film Preview	7.30 Coronation Street	9.00 ER	8.30 In the Dark
9.00 Nine o'clock News	9.30 Crossing the Lines	8.00 Animal Survival	10.00 Drop the Dead Donkey	9.00 Film
9.30 Out of Hours	10.20 10 × 10	10.00 News	10.30 Who's Line Is It Anyway?	10.30 Melinda's Big Night In
10.00 Holiday Quest	10.30 Newsnight	10.30 International Football	11.00 King of the Hill	11.00 American Ice Hockey

Fill in the times.

a) *Brookside* starts at ☐.☐☐ on _____ .

b) *Coronation Street* started at ☐.☐☐ and finished at ☐.☐☐ .

c) Write out the times of the news on each channel.

Fill in the number of minutes.

d) *The Pepsi Chart* lasts ☐ minutes.

e) *Neighbours* lasts ☐ minutes.

f) *ER* lasts ☐ minutes.

18 Answer **Yes** or **No**. If you had a one-hour tape could you tape:

a) *The Pepsi Chart* and *Home and Away*?

b) *Animal Survival* and *Tonight*?

c) *Coronation Street* and *Emmerdale*?

d) *Star Trek* and *Party of Five*?

UNIT 12 MEASURES

19 Write down five different ways you could use a one-hour tape to record some programmes.
Use the programmes above or your own list of programmes.
You could tape just **one** programme or **more** than one.
Each time you must use **as much** of the hour as possible.

20 Try Worksheet Puzzle *Plan a timetable*.

Now try Unit 12 Test.

Review 12

1 Put in order – **smallest** number first.
16   1063   10 006   106   1406

2 Write the money as **decimals**.

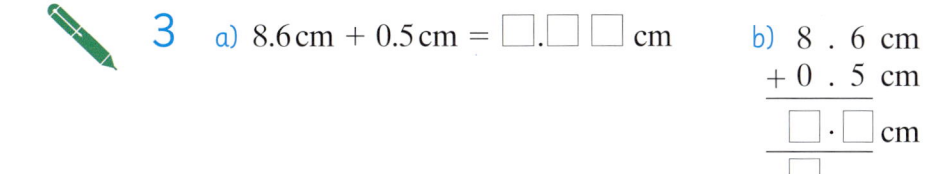

a)

£☐.☐☐

b)

c)

3 a) 8.6 cm + 0.5 cm = ☐.☐☐ cm   b) 8 . 6 cm
                                     + 0 . 5 cm
                                     ─────────
                                       ☐ . ☐ cm
                                       ☐

4 a)   2 5 7   b)   1 8 2   c)   1 1 8   d)   5 6 2
     +   5 4   −   4 5   + 8 3 6   − 4 9 2
     ───────   ───────   ───────   ───────

   e)   2 4 6   f)   7 0 5   g)   5 3 8   h)   7 0 6
     + 2 9 2   − 5 5 7   + 4 6 2   − 1 4 3
     ───────   ───────   ───────   ───────

            £☐.☐☐   £☐.☐☐

5 A quarter ($\frac{1}{4}$) of:

   a) £8 → ☐   b) £28 → ☐   c) £32 → £☐

   d) £8.40 → £☐   e) £28.12 → £☐   f) £32.24 → ☐